D1528747

DURING SLEEP

Other books by the author

Case-Book of Astral Projection, 545-746
Out-of-the-Body Experiences: A Fourth Analysis
The Study and Practice of Astral Projection

DURING SLEEP

The possibility of "co-operation"
between the living and the dead.

by

ROBERT CROOKALL
B.Sc. (Psychology), D.Sc., Ph.D.

Foreword by Leslie Shepard

UNIVERSITY BOOKS INC.   SECAUCUS, NEW JERSEY

Printed in U.S.A. by
NOBLE OFFSET PRINTERS, INC.
New York, N.Y. 10003

FOREWORD TO AMERICAN EDITION

DR. ROBERT CROOAKLL has already established a world-wide reputation for his brilliant studies of the phenomenon of Astral Projection or out-of-the-body traveling. Many of his books have been issued by University Books Inc.

In this new book he develops the findings of these earlier studies to establish the reality of a much wider field—the survival of the soul after death, and the possibilities of *co-operation* between living and dead souls.

Dr. Crookall presents strong suggestive evidence that such co-operation helps the living, the newly-dead in passing over, and *earthbound* spirits that are attached to worldly emotions even after death. This book therefore enormously extends the findings of out-of-the-body traveling into areas of psychical science, spiritualism and religion.

In his earlier books Dr. Crookall showed how the validation of out-of-the-body traveling necessarily involved basic concepts of a vital body (*vehicle of vitality*) and a soul body, in addition to the physical body of everyday life. These concepts, which have brought clarity and order to an understanding of the principles and laws governing astral projection, are equally illuminating in areas formerly covered by traditional religions.

Christianity and pagan religions alike have always stressed the reality of the human soul and its evolution after death. A modern world, almost wholly preoccupied with materialistic preoccupations of this life has tended to scoff at the old religious teachings about the soul as mere superstitious folklore, but in this present book Dr. Crookall demonstrates that the old religious beliefs may have a satisfactory scientific basis. While the evidence may not yet be irrefutable, it is at least consistent and convincing. It meets the facts, and provides a basis for further detailed investigation.

Dr. Crookall claims that one of the most important periods in our lifetime for co-operation between the souls of the living and the dead is *during sleep.* Sleep is a much more complex and mysterious condition than most of us believe, and is certainly much more than a mere resting period from the strains of walking life. In his earlier books Dr. Crookall showed how during sleep the astral body or vehicle of vitality may travel outside the physical body, visit distant places and return with information formerly ascribed (rather unsatisfactorily) to *telepathy.* The evidence for the reality of this phenomenon rests firmly upon hundreds of firsthand accounts by individuals from all walks of life, as described in many books on astral projection by Dr. Crookall and other writers.

But Dr. Crookall now shows that the individual may also enter the soul body—a much more subtle body than the vehicle of vitality, and visit spirit realms characterized by religious teachings of heaven and hell. In all these travels, astral or spiritual, the individual may be helped or hindered by other living souls, by the souls of the dead, and even by angelic and demonic spirits. Dr. Crookall stresses the positive side of such *co-operation,* in which spiritually advanced souls may help those others who have passed over without proper preparation, wandering in confusion or despair in strange other worlds. Living souls, temporarily outside the physical body during sleep may also be helped by co-operators from spiritual realms. But there are also sinister implications of possible *co-operation* between evil souls and demonic forces.

On this latter point I personally have no doubt that the tremendous eruption of evil and destruction which is so characteristic of modern life cannot be ascribed simply to living human beings of our own generation, but rather demonstrates how living men and women may attract evil forces from beyond this life. One need only point to the sickening horrors of the Nazi concentration camps, and the continuing tide of cruelty, violence, destruction and degeneration that has flooded the postwar affluent society.

It follows that all men and women of goodwill who realize the tremendous power of positive *co-operation* between each other, with noble spirits who have passed over, and with divine forces from beyond this life, may yet combine to bring about a renaissance of peace, justice, kindness and spiritual awareness.

This book therefore has tremendous implications far beyond the mere novelty of traveling outside one's physical body during sleep. If more people can begin to study the great forces at work in the universe, and the importance of mutual *co-operation* in positive evolution of different souls, life will have a deeper meaning and a greater joy.

This is the first American edition of a work originally published in Britain. It comes opportunely at a time when thousands of individuals need the inspiration and wisdom that comes from a proper analysis of the mysterious phenomena of life. The modern explosion of interest in the occult has been a reaction against narrow materialism stemming from an improved science. But much of occultism is unfortunately only materialism in a new guise—the desire for power and influence over others, with spells and witchcraft rituals instead of stock exchange manipulations and all the shoddy tricks of the selfish property game. It is important to remember that the true message of the occult is the secret knowledge of life beyond the limitations of everyday life, the meaning and purpose of man's evolution.

So often in everyday life one traps oneself in the limitations of the body and senses by narrow egocentric desires and ambitions, by greed, selfishness, and negative emotions. Out-of-the-body traveling may lead us to stranger regions than the physical world. The message of this book is that there are heavens and hells beyond death, that the purpose of life is the perfection of the soul beyond this first frontier of the physical body. That at every moment each individual soul stands before eternity.

This has always been the teaching of the great religions, and if they have differed in detail and dogma, nevertheless the essential basis has remained the same, and has inspired countless souls throughout history.

In this remarkable book, Dr. Crookall reminds us of inescapable truths of destiny, and shows us that religion may also be a matter of science.

1973   LESLIE SHEPARD

PREFACE

MOST people regard the matters considered here as fantastic. That attitude is not surprising in a world that is so thoroughly materialistic. Nevertheless, as Solomon (Prov. xviii, 13) pointed out, "He that answereth a matter *before he heareth it*, it is a shame and a folly unto him." If there should prove to be truth in this matter, then it is profoundly important, both to individual men and women and to humanity at large.

Since, unless the "mind" or "soul" survives the death of the physical body, "co-operation", the subject of this study, is impossible, a few observations are necessary on that subject.

The evidence for survival is of two kinds, direct and indirect. The direct, or specific, evidence is considered in a number of excellent books, including G. N. M. Tyrrell's *Human Personality* (Pelican Books, 1946), Hereward Carrington's *Psychic Science and Survival* (Two Worlds Publishing Co. Ltd., 1939), Dr R. C. Johnson's *Psychical Research* (English Universities Press Ltd., 1955), Rosalind Heywood's *The Sixth Sense* (Chatto & Windus, 1959) and W. H. Salter's *Zoar* (Sidgwick & Jackson, 1961). By far the best and most up-to-date expositions are those by Professor Hornell Hart (*The Enigma of Survival*, Rider & Co. Ltd., 1959), Professor C. J. Ducasse (*A Critical Examination of the Belief in a Life after Death*, Thomas, U.S.A., 1961), and Dr S. Ralph Harlow (*A Life after Death*, 1961). An excellent selection of cases was given by A. T. Baird in his *A Casebook for Survival* (Psychic Press Ltd.).

The present writer has considered certain indirect, or inferential, evidence for survival in *The Supreme*

Adventure (James Clarke & Co. Ltd., 1961) and *The Study and Practice of Astral Projection* (Aquarian Press, 1961). Although the results cannot be coercive, they supplement those based on the direct evidence.

The direct evidence for survival approaches (though it fails to attain) actual demonstration. It is vitiated by the possibility that it may merely represent an admixture (in various proportions) of (1) dramatization (in which an incarnate soul unconsciously adopts the rôle and acts the part of a discarnate soul); (2) dissociation within the total mind of the incarnate soul (with the separation of certain "sub-conscious" from "conscious" elements); and (3) psychic ability (chiefly telepathy and clairvoyance). It is important to note that the indirect evidence for survival, e.g. that based on (*a*) "communications" descriptive of the experiences undergone during transition; (*b*) certain observations made by nurses, doctors and others at death-beds; (*c*) certain descriptions of clairvoyants; (*d*) the deductions made by certain philosophers; (*e*) the deductions made by de Bary (who had out-of-the-body experiences) are all entirely unaffected by the three above-mentioned factors. The indirect evidence that is adduced by Dr Ian Stevenson, M.D., in his study entitled *Evidence for Survival from Claimed Memories of Former Incarnations* (obtainable for 2*s*. 4*d*. from M. C. Peto, 16 Kingswood Road, Tadworth, Surrey) is also unaffected by these possibilities. When both direct and indirect evidence are considered, survival, though not "scientifically proved", is a practical certainty.

R. CROOKALL

"He that answereth a matter before he heareth it, it is a shame and a folly unto him."—*Solomon.*

"We know almost nothing about deep sleep. . . . It is towards deep sleep that psychologists should direct their efforts in order not only to study the mechanism of the unconscious memory, but also to examine the more mysterious phenomena relating to physical research."—*Professor Henri Bergson.*

"Sleep is not due to physiological brain-changes, but the withdrawal of the 'Soul' or 'Ego'—call it what you will— from the everyday world. In this way it seeks communion with the primordial rhythm of life. . . . The secret of safe-passage through the shoals of 'the world beyond the visible' is to have some object to achieve in the world of today. Then life will be energized by an excursion among the intangibles, just as it is by periods of restful, natural sleep which serve the same purpose—that of re-charging the run-down battery of life."—*Dr William Wilson.*

"The ancient idea that man is a microcosm, or little world, in himself, developing in response to the Macrocosm, or Universe, and having its counterpart in his own being, is a far more adequate conception than the prevailing attempt to envisage man as an evolving animal."—*Dr J. Parton Milum.*

CONTENTS

INTRODUCTION

The Psalmist (cxxviii, 2) stated: "He giveth his beloved *during* sleep." Certain moderns who regard sleep-time as wasted time, recommend its curtailment. The present writer considers it at least as important as our waking hours. Each of the two phases, sleeping and waking, is necessary for a full and fruitful life.

The Church repeats the statement of the Psalmist with little, if any, awareness that it has profound and far-reaching implications. This is related to its attitude towards several closely related topics of great importance (see Appendix I).

There is much to suggest that the function of sleep does not end with bodily rest from mental activity, that, in addition, it permits the soul to obtain refreshment and encouragement by way of "visits" to the "next world", i.e. it facilitates out-of-the-body experiences or astral projections. In addition it provides. conditions in which one can (and many do) help other mortals, the dying, the newly-dead, etc. These latter activities constitute "co-operation".

We first assemble and classify (without, of course, prejudging) numerous statements and testimonies concerning "co-operation" from four independent sources. These are astral projectors, psychics, the dying (who were psychic) and supposed "communicators", then correlate the statements and testimonies with the observations and conclusions of psychical researchers, etc.

DURING SLEEP

CHAPTER I

"CO-OPERATION" AS DESCRIBED BY ASTRAL PROJECTORS

1. "CO-OPERATION" THAT HELPS OTHER MORTALS

MRS CLARA CLAYTON, of Nottingham, stated (*in litt.*):
"I had gone to bed but not fallen asleep, and felt myself
[Soul Body][1] slipping out. I found myself with a mother
and her babe. They were in bed. A state of distress
showed in her aura and I became aware that she was
calling for her husband. I soothed her until she ceased
to weep, and then soothed her to sleep. But she did not
see me as the dying ones (whom I had helped) had done.
*Almost at once I saw the 'sea'; this 'sea' was the Astral World
[='Hades'], the world of emotion. I saw one coming across
the 'sea' and realized it was the husband. I assisted the mother
to leave her physical body and she stood beside me in her Astral
[=Soul] Body and became aware of me. With a great cry, she
saw her husband.* They embraced and the happiness
which they felt glowed through them. When in her
physical body, her loved one could not make her aware
of him because of her great grief; but once out of her
body, he was able to meet her in the Astral World
['Hades'—intermediate between earth and 'Paradise'].
She would wake out of that 'dream', as she would call
it, and remember having seen her husband. This might
be enough to stop her grieving—her 'dream' would
have been very vivid and so would be stamped in her

[1] Explanations and comments inserted by the present writer are
given in square brackets.

memory for ever. ... Grief prevents our loved ones manifesting to us; it also keeps them near the earth and this retards their progress."

2. "CO-OPERATION" THAT HELPS THE DYING

Mrs Clayton stated (*in litt.*): "I had only just closed my eyes and had slipped out of my body and found myself, with others, waiting for the 'passing' of a soul, first that of a lady and second a little boy. We soothed them and waited for the process of dying to come to an end, and we bore them to their spiritual abode [='Paradise'] to rest awhile. The mourners did not see us, but both the lady and the boy became aware of us [=deathbed 'visions'] and they lost the fear of death."

3. "CO-OPERATION" THAT HELPS THE NEWLY-DEAD

Miss Hillier, of Croydon, said (*in litt.*) that, during sleep, she finds herself [in the Soul Body] where people have just been killed in some disaster. She stated: "I lead them to their [discarnate] relatives. ... Later I read of such a disaster in the newspapers. I cannot explain why I am called upon to do this work [of 'co-operation']."

A Mr Emerson's experience was described by Dr Horace Leaf, PH.D., F.R.G.S., in *Light* (LV, 1935, p. 86). When in Australia, he "left his body" at the request of his (discarnate) sister and eventually found his cousin who had died a few months before. This cousin was "a firm believer that the dead sleep until the Judgement Day". Emerson's sister explained the situation to him as follows: "He was a good man, but we are unable to awaken him [because of this fixed idea]. You try!"

When the cousin showed signs of awakening, Emerson had to leave.

An Englishwoman, Mrs Olive Mytton-Hill (*in litt.*), gave a somewhat similar testimony. Although, soon after her husband died, she saw and spoke to him, he responded only very feebly. She said, "I immediately felt that he had been 'built-up' for just the occasion: he was depressed beyond hope. Immediately I got back [into the physical body] I thought, '*I was sent there to help him to realize where he was*' [='dead']."

Katherine Trevelyan (*Fool in Love*, Gollancz, 1960, p. 215) in her "clear dreams" [i.e. astral projections] was helping her father [who, having died in the firm belief that there is no after-life, had "put a spell" on himself that acted like post-hypnotic suggestion]. He could not leave his egotism, accept his daughter's love and move on. As she observed, "That is just what the sorrow of egotism is—it cannot unite with another." She saw souls "at different stages of development" and a young woman who was helping one of them. "This girl was doing for the soul after death," she observed, "what a physiotherapist might be doing for the body on earth. She said that *on earth she was an unimportant typist, but at night she did this work for those struggling in the darkness.* ... How often, sitting opposite her in the Underground, I might have summed her up as a nonentity: whereas actually she was called to very advanced work during the unconscious hours, of which, she had indicated, *she knew nothing during her life on earth.*"

4. "CO-OPERATION" THAT HELPS THE "EARTH-BOUND"

Mrs Clara Clayton, of Nottingham, said (*in litt.*): "I have had several vivid experiences of meeting loved ones who have passed away, and also of visiting other countries when in sleep. Here is an experience of going into one of the dark realms (='Hades'] to give assistance to one who dwelt there since his departure from the physical world. I was with a companion that night and I knew we were both functioning out-of-the-body and our mission was known to us. We glided downwards (so it seemed to my consciousness) and the atmosphere was becoming denser, and it seemed to me the light was going. There was a damp mist and a sensation of coldness [='Hades' conditions]. All this had to be overcome, as I had not experienced these things before. ... Then a light began to glow in the dark, heavy atmosphere and, with surprise, I realized it was coming from my companion and myself. Down and still down we seemed to go, far away from the Realm of Light [='Paradise']. Our destination was reached—a dark cavern in and out of which souls were passing, each apparently unaware of the other. They appeared dark, cold and miserable. Suddenly I became aware of one coming out who was completely isolated. We knew our task was with him. We each took an arm and lifted him up. He began to weep, and, as he wept, his 'garment' grew lighter: then he became conscious of us and smiled. We rose together, he being supported by us. We reached the top of a hill where a great assembly had gathered to greet this soul. The atmosphere here was brighter. *Suddenly I knew what to do. I went into the midst of the gathering and found his wife and child. They were united. ...* Help is always at hand, but these souls in darkness are unaware of the closeness of ministering angels; also the cry reaches us who are out of the body and *the task is often given to us ordinary folk to lift them up—they recognize us to be like themselves, just ordinary human beings."*

CHAPTER II

"CO-OPERATION" AS DESCRIBED BY PSYCHICS

1. "CO-OPERATION" THAT HELPS OTHER MORTALS

MARY E. MONTEITH (*The Fringe of Immortality*, John Murray, 1920, pp. 146, 195) said: "To the psychic, the importance of prayer is proved almost daily. Laying aside the numerous cases of sudden inspirations that certain individuals are in difficulties, or the unaccountable impulse to give some practical help in a quarter where, to judge by outward appearances, it is not necessary—*laying these aside as examples of purely telepathic significance [from incarnate souls], there is a preponderance of definite instructions of the requirements of certain individuals given by discarnate spirits.* When it is possible to act on these instructions, diplomatically, for it is seldom that one may give the true reason for practical interest, invariably the remark is made, '*All this has come as an answer to prayer!*'" *Her very considerable experience led her to conclude that "most adequate responses in practical matters are of this type".* She also maintained, "The psychic, to whom thought is a real and actual influence, a supremely powerful influence on human actions, the divine precept 'Men ought always to pray' (Luke xviii, I) has a definite meaning. It is pre-eminently practical. In my own experiences, and I repeat, mine is no isolated case, there is much that has forced my belief in prayer and on a purely logical basis. As mere thought, I find it an influence on human beings the extent of which none can gauge; the interchange of mental vibrations alone causes much happiness and unhappiness."

It is worthy of note that Miss Monteith's experience was that her psychic development depended chiefly on *concentration—not artificially-practised concentration, but "habitually, on every little thing in daily life"*. A balanced life was necessary and practical activities were not neglected. She said, *"Our co-operation had, as its object, to attain personal knowledge of the higher laws which could be practically brought to bear on earthly existence*. For a short time I had the inevitable suspicion of orthodox training that all this must be the devil. ... Looking back, I can most honestly testify that in every communication where co-operation has been necessary, *the desire to assuage the sufferings of humanity has been uppermost*."

Miss Monteith described how her interest was first aroused in psychic matters. She was given "imperative messages" that purported to come from a Dr Neil whom she had known during his lifetime. She was provided with "very decided proofs of his personality", some unknown to her at the time and verified only at a later date. The "doctor" asked to be allowed to use her hand to write. He told her to be critical. Soon she was able to verify a message the first part of which was written through the hand of a friend whose sister was with Miss Monteith at the time. The message was as follows: "There are people in distress at 3 Smith Street in this town. Tell Miss M. to go and see what she can do for them."

Miss Monteith, though very dubious, went to the address, which was in a poor part of the town, and found that the people had left for new quarters. She went there and a sad-looking woman opened the door. Her account continues, "I explained that a friend had told me that they were in trouble and I had come to help them. She invited me in and I had no difficulty in gaining her confidence. It was a sad case. Both she and her sister were very delicate and unable to get work. One had been trained for a profession but she had lost her posts through ill-health. ... They were not in a class to beg, and their natural reticence had brought them to a very low pass. ... There was no difficulty in helping them. ... Now they are well, happy and prosperous." This adventure in "co-operation" decided Miss Monteith to continue with her psychic work.

Another instance of "co-operation" in which "Dr Neil" and Miss Monteith were concerned was cited (op. cit., p. 9). "Dr Neil" asked her to make a point of knowing a certain Mrs Burton and try and interest her in the possibility of communication with those who had "passed on". She did as requested and found that Mrs Burton had mixed much with scientists and was profoundly sceptical as to all psychic matters and particularly as to the possibility of communication. Later, "Dr Neil", using Miss Monteith's hand, emphatically declared that Mrs Burton's husband, Major Burton, would soon die. He was, in fact, killed in the fighting in Mesopotamia. Soon after his death he communicated and gave what his wife described as "good proofs of his identity". It was evident that "Dr Neil" was aware of Major Burton's imminent death, as well as of Mrs Burton's excessive scepticism, and "co-operated" with Miss Monteith to help them both.

Miss Monteith herself received many "helpful inspirations" bearing on private affairs: at the time these entered her mind she felt the presence of certain friends who had died. Before she became convinced of survival and occasional communication, she regarded these "inspirations" as answers to prayer, and the sense of "presence" that accompanied them as due to imagination, but was later obliged to alter her views. She observed (op. cit., p. 98), "Psychic workers often receive messages actually indicating the whereabouts of people in distress, and help given for this reason is invariably said, *by the recipients,* to have come as a direct answer to prayer. Without denying the reality of thoughts (prayers), and the possibility of their being received unconsciously by one who is more attuned by *sympathetic interest* (Divine intervention through a natural law), *some individuals work in the light of conscious guidance from discarnate spirits, whose interest, anxiety and knowledge, apart from anything else, point to a relationship which death could not sever.*"

If one can help other mortals, one can also hinder them. Mrs Eileen J. Garrett (*My Life as a Search for the Meaning of Mediumship,* Rider & Co. Ltd., 1939, p. 15) when only a child made the same observation as Miss Monteith. She stated, "The impacts which I saw taking place in the 'surrounds' [vehicles of vitality] of people as they met and reacted to each other's thoughts and emotions, constantly disturbed me. I saw how people's conflicts rocked them without their understanding why, and I gradually became aware that *people were thus the unconscious victims of each other's moods.*"

In Stewart Edward White's *The Betty Book* (Psychic Book Club, 1945, p. 99) it is stated: "We are broadcasting even with our most secret thoughts and desires. We are accountable for what we send out. Our desire does not die in our breasts. It goes out as something we have launched, to run straight ahead on its appointed course until the force of its projection is exhausted, or until it meets a more powerful or deflecting force. It may be going and fulfilling its destiny long after we have forgotten it. That is part of our responsibility."

Mrs Garrett (*Telepathy,* Creative Press Inc., 1941,

p. 93) deprecated experiments in telepathy that consist merely of "games" and "guessing". She said, "Out of my own vast experience of daily living, I have seen the telepathic understanding, when used from higher motive, expand vast areas of consciousness, and draw from the creative self hitherto unsuspected strength in colour and harmony, and finally in self-healing. ... With the help of telepathy ... I have effectively changed the *sensori stimuli* of the weak, the distressed and the ill. ... All forms of mental attitude can be changed. ... Fatigue and confusion are lessened. As soon as one allows a patient to feel that he has, within his own hallucinations and visions, a means to help himself, he will receive other impressions in place of his own. You have created a new world of understanding for him." Here Mrs Garrett "co-operated" with other mortals to their mutual advantage.

Dr Annie Besant (*Man's Life in This and Other Worlds*, Theosophical Publishing House, 1913, p. 42) gave the following suggestion: "You know someone who is in trouble, in the grip of a vice, etc. Think of him as you go to sleep—think that you want to go to him and to comfort him. Your thought will carry you to him when you fall asleep and you will give him the comfort that you desire. Many a vice has been broken in that way, for in the hours of sleep, when a man is more susceptible than at any other times [his Soul Body is not then insulated by the physical body], you may go to him astrally [=in the Soul Body] and put to him the arguments which, in his waking state, would anger him. In the astral that thought can be printed on his mind and *it will come to him as his own thinking when he wakes*." Dr Besant continued as follows: "And so with those you love who have passed away from you in death, sometimes you dream of them. You do not realize that it is no dream; it is a real meeting in the world into which you go when your body is asleep. *Think of your loved dead, fix your mind on them, and in the hours of [bodily] sleep you, waking, shall be with them and may give them much help.* As you develop you become 'awake' on the astral plane [here='Paradise'] ... your astral senses are turned outwards. You see, feel, hear, know and can talk more freely than here. And when there is some calamity, such as an earthquake, ship-wreck or war, *if you will you can be a helper*—you can be there to help those unhappy ones feeling out of their bodies; you may go to them calming and consoling. And when you have that consciousness, death ceases to alarm, for this world into which we go every night in sleep [='Paradise'] is the same world into which we pass after death. Some Christians call it 'the intermediate world', intermediate between this world and Heaven."

Alice A. Bailey (*The Externalization of the Hierarchy*, Lucis Press, 1958) distinguished between psychics of a "low order" (who may do harm, both to themselves and others) and those of a "high order". The latter, she said, "give themselves so that their fellow men may learn of them." She concluded, "*Thus, on both sides of the veil of separation are souls aided and given opportunity to heal and serve.*"

2. "CO-OPERATION" THAT HELPS THE DYING

Mrs Gladys Osborn Leonard (*The Last Crossing*, Psychic Book Club, 1937, p. 73) deprecated attempts by undertakers to keep a corpse as lifelike as possible since the means employed may delay the complete release of the vehicle of vitality and the severance of the "silver cord". (See *The Supreme Adventure*, by the present writer,

pp. 120, 130, 188.) She described how she "co-operated"
in one such case. The corpse had been "treated", i.e.
"preserved", and she could see clairvoyantly that the
"cord" was unsevered. She prayed for help and three
discarnate helpers ("deliverers") appeared. Mrs
Leonard told them that she would do their bidding.
Her account continues: "I then felt impelled to make
upward 'passes' and, while concentrating on the cord
being severed, I made several 'passes' along the body
from the feet towards the head. I was impressed to start
near the solar plexus [to which the cord of the vehicle of
vitality is attached—whereas the 'cord' of the Soul
Body is attached to the head] and continued them well
beyond the head. ... After ten minutes I felt a sense of
relief. ... The 'astral cord' had been broken, leaving the
soul free. ..."

3. "CO-OPERATION" THAT HELPS THE NEWLY-DEAD (AWAKENING "SLEEPERS", ETC.)

According to many independent "communicators",
men of average type have an after-death sleep (see the
writer's *The Supreme Adventure*, James Clarke & Co. Ltd.,
1961, pp. 133, 139). The sleep-period may, however,
be prolonged for various reasons. In the first place, men
who have deliberately and persistently declared that
there is no after-life or that one sleeps until the "Day of
Judgement" may have laid something corresponding
to a post-hypnotic suggestion upon themselves: they
may, therefore, fail to awaken at the proper time.
Others definitely want to avoid facing their "Judgement"-experience (see the writer's *The Supreme Adventure*, pp. 42, 173). People who belong to these cate-
gories are often brought to "rescue circles" (op. cit.
1961, pp. 162, 235).

Arthur Ford (*Nothing So Strange*, Harper, 1958, p. 164), after mentioning the after-death sleep, said: "*Some individuals wish to sleep: they do not want to face whatever reckoning lies before them.* Apparently, however, the sleeping dead can be wakened to their new reality by the *loving prayers* of the living, indeed it seems that *they are often more easily reached by a living person than a discarnate.*" Again (p. 225): "I am convinced that much that we call *inspiration* is really *co-operation* between minds willing to share both ideas and energy. Their joint effort is telepathic, but it has to be with intent to further a common end, even though intention does not reach the threshold of consciousness. ... This is the way of accomplishing God's larger purposes. *Moreover, this pooling of effort and aspiration may include both incarnate and discarnate persons.*"

Still again (p. 246)—"Survival is not the only tenet of the Gospel, but it is the one without which the others lose much of their significance. One has only to see the transformation in the lives of some who suddenly realize that personality is not lost in death to know how basic the assurance is. Likewise, one has only to experience the co-operation of unseen presences still animated by love and dedicated to service, to know that the company of the righteous is invincible."

H. A. Curtis and Dr F. H. Curtis (*Realms of the Living Dead*, 1917, p. 61) spoke of people who died strongly believing there is no after-life and who therefore slept for an unduly long time after death and were difficult to awaken. They said, "This, among many other tasks, is the work assigned to those students who, during sleep on earth, have *asked* to be put to work in the astral [here='Hades'] world. Many of us would be surprised could we remember all tasks performed during sleep."

The exceptionally able clairvoyant C. W. Leadbeater

(*Invisible Helpers*, T.P.S., 3rd ed., 1917) said: "Many of the departed who wish to help the friends whom they have left behind find themselves unable to influence them since they lack the necessary knowledge and skill, while their friends lack sensitiveness. Hence, little help is usually given by the [average] dead—indeed it is far more common for them to be themselves in need of assistance than to be able to give it to others. ... *The bulk of the work which has to be done along these lines falls to the lot of living persons who are able to function consciously on the astral plane* [here = 'Paradise' conditions]."

4. "CO-OPERATION" THAT HELPS THE "EARTHBOUND"

E. A. Tietkens (*Mediumistic and Psychical Experiences*, L.S.A., Ltd.) said: "Before waking up and regaining consciousness I see with my spiritual eyes that I am surrounded by many living individualities. They are not bad people, but those who are still guided by mortal tastes and loves. They do not entertain any further aspirations. Can this be a means of utilizing a medium's spirit to help to raise the earthbound spirits—preaching to them in prison, so to say? ... I am impressed that *these individuals receive through my mediumship a higher spiritual state of being, helped to it by my guides.* ... Imbibing this higher aura, they are able to rise spiritually."

Olive B. Pixley (*The Trail*, The C. W. Daniel Co. Ltd., 1934) said: "Megalomaniacs are quite happy in thinking themselves all that their fancy paints them. Where—when their spirits leave their bodies—can their minds go? Only to their favourite haunts of illusion on the astral plane [= 'Hades']. ... If we know how to radiate the power of love into the spirits on the astral plane, to make them aware of Reality, we can direct their minds from illusion towards the realities of the World of Light [='Paradise'].''

5. "CO-OPERATION" THAT HELPS COMMUNICATION

H. A. Curtis and Dr F. H. Curtis (op. cit., 1917, p. 92) stated that "The inhabitants of this ['Paradise'] realm can see the physical conditions of their mortal friends only when those friends are thinking about [=mentally 'calling'] them and sending them their magnetism [=substance from the vehicle of vitality], or, when the necessary earthly magnetism [ditto] is furnished by a medium. In all cases, communication is easier if the mortals send the 'departed' ones *love and sympathy*, also if they know something of life-after-death. *Mortals can therefore be of the greatest help to their loved ones who have 'passed on' by familiarizing themselves with spiritual truths—not merely dabbling in phenomena. For if a mental call is sent out to the loved ones, they will come and study with the mortal and thus rapidly learn the explanation of the problems which confront them in the higher life. ... In return, they can make it easier for the mortal loved ones to grasp them.*''

CHAPTER III

"CO-OPERATION" AS DESCRIBED BY THE DYING (WHO WERE PSYCHIC)

"CO-OPERATION" THAT HELPS THE "EARTHBOUND"

IN the life of Frau Hauffe, the "Seeress of Prevorst", published in 1829 by her medical adviser, a man of exceptional ability, statements identical with the above are made. Frau Hauffe was "more than half dead" [=with the vehicle of vitality more than half released] for years prior to her actual transition. During that period she saw, and conversed with, many persons in the "earthbound" condition [=with the vehicle of vitality still accompanying the Soul Body]. She said: *"They come to me that I may aid them through prayer and give them a word of consolation. ..."* This lady (who had very little education) realized that there was a greater "vibrational gulf" between the "angels" [in the Soul Body and "Paradise" conditions] and her unfortunate "earthbound" visitors [in "Hades"] than between the "earthbound" and herself. She said, *"Their weight [='semi-physical' vehicle of vitality] draws them more to men than to spirits."* Asked why they approached her rather than other mortals, she replied that she was "so constituted that they could naturally see and hear each other" [i.e. that, owing to the state of her health, her vehicle of vitality was more than half released]. The fact that she could see these unfortunate discarnate Souls she regarded as the great misfortune of her life. She said, "When asleep, I rejoice to live amongst the

Spirits [in 'Paradise'] but awake, they [the 'earthbound' in 'Hades'] make me sad." Since people would not believe what she described, she was "deserted and misunderstood". The case of Frau Hauffe in Germany should be compared with that of Daisy Dryden, an American child of ten, who similarly lingered between life and death—in this case for three days (see *Journ.*, A.S.P.R., xii, No. 6). Daisy also saw and conversed with the "living dead" and it is significant that she did *not* contact the "earthbound".

We repeat the statements and testimonies cited above are neither accepted nor rejected. Whether there is *evidence* that they may have some correspondence to fact will be considered later.

CHAPTER IV

"CO-OPERATION" AS DESCRIBED BY COMMUNICATORS

THE following "communications" are here merely quoted: *the possibility that they may have some evidential support is considered later.*

The "communications" were obtained through mediums. Since they are identical with the statements of non-mediums, i.e. of astral projectors, of psychics, and of the dying, they cannot be dismissed as sub-conscious productions of the mediums concerned.

Moreover, whereas none of the astral projectors, the psychics or the dying provided any reasonable explanation of the phenomenon which we call "co-operation", many "communicators" do this—they either suggest or actually indicate that "co-operative" activities depend upon that "semi-physical" portion of our total bodily condition which we term the vehicle of vitality. This is one of the many answers to those who have jibed "communicators"—"Tell us something we don't know!"

1. "CO-OPERATION" THAT HELPS OTHER MORTALS

Nearly a century ago, the "communicator" of *Life Beyond the Grave*, E. W. Allen, 1876, p. 40 stated: "We pray for help, let the object be what it may, but not if it be an evil object. In the latter case prayer certainly is undesirable, for it is the cause of attracting to you spirits who will aid you in accomplishing your purpose, perhaps, but they will only increase your unhappiness afterwards; for if you have strong will-power, *you are tempting them*! On the other hand, if you pray for a good object, you benefit the spirits whom you draw around you. It is good for them to help others, and in helping you, they help themselves. Thus, you see, prayer is a spiritual force. ... It is something like advertising your wants in the newspapers. ... *You should, of course, pray to God, not to spirit. He permits spirits to execute His decrees. ... Earnest longing for help is the true prayer.*"

The "communicator" of M. Hoey (*Truths from the Spirit World*, 1907, p. 97) insisted that prayers should be definite and not vague, adding, "Does it surprise you that *some of us [discarnate souls] are permitted to answer prayers?* It is, indeed, a task of love set us by the Father to attend to the *physical and mental needs* of His children."

"Claude" (*Claude's Second Book*, Methuen & Co. Ltd., 1919, p. 121) similarly said, "*God uses discarnate spirits to do His work*, to help, comfort and direct those on earth".

The "communicator" of Kate Wingfield (*Guidance from Beyond*, Philip Allen, 1923, p. 35) observed: "The more the heart feels its own helplessness to act individually, the more it breathes itself out in prayer and draws to itself the powers that encompass it about; *and so it is that one may be the centre for many unseen intelligences to work through.*" Later (*More Guidance from Beyond*, Philip Allen & Co. Ltd., 1925, p. 13) she was told: "A smile, a word, is enough—if the heart goes with it. You can do so much more than you can ever know in that way. *Many will come to you to be helped, both on your side and on ours.* ... Sometimes it is hard for you to realize that you are helping souls on the other side— but it is true all the same. Even the wish to help formed strongly in your mind, is help in itself. Your spirit-actions are far more reaching-forward than you realize. And what you think of in the body and wish to do but cannot, *you can very often perform when you get on the other side, even when you are still in the body* [=*chiefly during sleep*]*. When a strong feeling of pity for someone possesses you—whether in the body or out of the body—your guides see your desire* [=*it is a 'call' to them*] *and fulfil for you what you cannot do for yourself."*

"Muriel", the "communicator" of Geraldine Cummins (*Travellers in Eternity*, Psychic Press Ltd., 1948, p. 171) transmitted the statement that discarnate souls who are in "Paradise" conditions [i.e. who have shed the vehicle of vitality] "can call in a group of people here *if we are asked by someone on earth to do so. But they are only permitted to work at the request of the living.*" She went on to mention the need for "the call"—"Will you, each night, for five minutes or so, think of Ruth and the group of healers, asking from your heart that they will go to Hilda and help her? For it is Ruth who is already in touch with them. ... *Certain groups of people of power and authority may, in some cases, help people on earth. But there has to be an urgent request* [='*Call*'] *made— that is the meaning of prayer.*"

"Muriel" also (op. cit., p. 177) said that she could not reach (the discarnate) "Harold" unless she got in touch with him "near the earth". In accomplishing this, mortals [who, it should be noted, possess the vehicle of vitality] had to "co-operate". Miss Gibbes, the recorder of the "communications", observed, "*Apparently contact through Geraldine and myself made this possible.*"

The "communicator" of G. G. André (*Morning Talks with Spirit Friends*, Watkins, 1926, p. 89) urged him to recognize the good in his brother man and to send him "*a ray of love which may serve as a channel of communication through which beneficient forces from the spirit-world may reach him*". Again (op. cit., p. 124) "Keep yourself consciously attached to the Source of your being. Be open to inspiration. Be a channel of communication between the loftier spheres and your brethren whose sight is still limited by the thick veil of the material body."

Still again, André was told: "Answers to your prayers may come through the ministrations of your guardian angels, guides and risen loved ones. ... They are God's agents to do His will concerning you. Theirs to enlighten, comfort and to encourage. ... *It is, for the most part, through the agency of ministering spirits that answers to your prayers come. But you must ask. You must know what you want with sufficient clearness to be able to put your question in definite terms.* A vague sense of need is not sufficient. ... Through the power you possess to attract the helpful companionship of spirit-friends, you may receive answers to prayer for Divine guidance; for they are His messengers to do His will. Therefore, through them His response to your appeal may come."

The Revd. C. Drayton Thomas (*Precognition and Human Survival*, Psychic Press Ltd., p. 80) was informed by a lady whose deceased son had given messages at his sittings, "Curious little things happen to me which I have put down as direct answers to prayer, and yet *I have wondered sometimes whether it is one of my loved ones helping me.*" Mr Thomas said, "My (deceased) sister had long ago described how plans were made in the higher spheres and thence passed to those whose work lay with earth." He pointed out that "*some of the plans made in the beyond require human co-operation*", that "human minds have to be impressed". Again, "When we pray 'Thy Kingdom come', do we not visualize some sort of unseen guidance in human affairs? Conceivably such guidance may be exerted by the Great Mind behind all creation; equally it is conceivable that God carries out His purposes by 'ministering spirits, servants of His who do His pleasure', among whom are some 'we loved and lost'."

The Revd. G. Maurice Elliott (*Angels Seen Today*, Elliott, 1919, p. 10), who, being occasionally clairvoyant, spoke from experience, pointed out, "There is no absolute dividing-line between this world and the next [='Paradise']. We are all carefully linked in a chain that stretches from lowest earth to highest heaven." Mr. Elliott continued: "St. Paul knew this and said (Eph. vi, 12) 'Our fight is not against human forces, but against ... the superhuman forces of evil in the heavens.' Prayers for the dead help them to ascend higher. *And we must especially pray for our tempter.*"

The "communicator" of Mary Bruce Wallace (*The Coming Light*, Watkins, 1924, p. 19) stated that spiritually-minded mortals (especially if also more or less psychic) can reach and help other mortals more readily than discarnate souls who are in "Paradise" conditions. The latter souls, he said, were "unable to come into close touch" with mortals (especially non-psychic mortals, since they were "screened" from them, by the physical body, at least during their waking hours. In *The Thinning of the Veil* (Watkins, 1919, p. 92) she was told that when we go to sleep we should expect more than physical and mental rest: "Regard yourself as starting upon a voyage into the Unknown: look for new experiences. *During sleep Heavenly Ones waken any who is ready to participate actively with their work. Those still in the physical body are able to influence sleepers better than the Heavenly Ones.*" The "communicator" further stated that discarnate souls are always "awakening" mortals who are sufficiently advanced psychically and spiritually to facilitate "co-operation" in various ways. On p. 62, he mentioned work especially with men who "passed" suddenly in war [and who therefore temporarily retained the vehicle of vitality and were in "Hades"]. He stated, "We have the greatest difficulty in arousing

such souls to any degree of interest in the life here
[='Paradise']. They are constantly wishing for the
past. ..."

G. Welsford (*Key of Gold*, The Society of Communion)
was informed, "When a soul still living on earth can be
awakened to spiritual laws, *he is used by the Angelic Rulers
to work among the 'poor' and 'blind' of earth. ... It is much
easier for you, who still possess physical bodies [which include
the vehicle of vitality], to do the work we long to do.*"

"Mr Sewall" (May Wright Sewall, *Neither Dead nor
Sleeping*, Watkins, 1921, p. 304) made the following
statement: "*The trouble with us, in our efforts to help you,
is that we are so tenuous. We cannot hold together; we need
your* [?ectoplasmic] *help* [from the vehicle of vitality] to get
the instruments that we can use." He estimated that
the thoughts of a disembodied soul "travel" twenty
times as fast as those of a physically-embodied soul. If
so, we may deduce that the thoughts and feelings of
mortals are twenty times as *powerful* as those of the
"dead".

The discarnate "Heslop" (*Speaking Across the Border-
line*, Charles Taylor, 1912, p. 24) reminded his incarnate wife that the New Testament is full of advice
to combine, i.e. "co-operate", in prayer—"When two
of you shall agree to ask anything ..." (Matt. xviii, 19);
"Where two or three are gathered together in my
Name ..." (Matt. xviii, 20), etc.—and stated, "When
we come to you from our side, it is in this spirit we come
—to help to raise your thought and sustain it as you
pray, and *to blend our petitions with yours.*" He continued,
"*There is no question of interposing ourselves to you in God's
stead.*"

Later (op. cit., p. 61) "Heslop" insisted that "the
highest spiritual gifts can only be developed by co-
operation on this side" [i.e. from high "Paradise"

conditions]. He pointed out that mortals who desire communication for material purposes, curiosity or amusement contact "wandering, border [-land] spirits, i.e. "earthbound" souls who are in "Hades" conditions. He warned: "To use psychic gifts so is to debase them." Harm often results from this. "But," he continued, "if the nature is spiritual, longing for fuller light and revelation, willing to live the higher and purer life, and to submit to steady discipline, then the higher spirits will always respond to such an one, and help to develop the psychic nature." He summed up the situation thus: "A pure and spiritual psychic may be able, literally, to bring heaven down to earth, because of the noble spirits who surround [and 'co-operate' with] him."

The "communicator" of W. S. Montgomery Smith (*Life and Work in the Spiritual Body*, Hillside Press) made a number of references to "co-operation". On p. 14 he (like many others) said that *love is the strongest link* [=*"call"*] *between mortals and discarnate souls.* This, he stated, "will afford the widest opportunity for transmission of important messages, besides conducing to their accurate delivery. We are urging you on, every one of us who has a connecting-link with your side. We work through that link. *It is the only way we can work for the benefit of mortals. ... Love enables people to contact each other after physical death.* There must be love to have perfect communication and co-operation in work, especially constructive work."

The discarnate "Wilberforce" (*Letters from the Other Side*, Watkins, 1919, p. 13) was asked if he was still "in touch" with an incarnate friend, "C"? He replied that "He comes here [into 'Paradise' conditions] during [his] sleep" when "we exchange manifestations of affection."

In France, P. E. Cornillier (*The Survival of the Soul*,

Kegan Paul, Trench, Trubner & Co. Ltd., 1921) gave several examples of "co-operation" that correspond with those mentioned by Geraldine Cummins. On p. 198 he mentioned trying to contact a (discarnate) "old friend" of his wife's. He succeeded and received proofs of identity. The "old friend" told Cornillier that contact and communication had proved difficult since he had passed far from earth conditions [into high "Paradise" conditions]. It had, however, been made possible by two conditions: first, the mortals had deliberately directed their thoughts towards [= "called"] him and secondly, *"the presence of the medium"* [*who possessed a vehicle of vitality that was "loose"*]. These two factors, one mental and the other bodily, combined to make "an effective force". [In this case the "co-operation" was necessary between medium and a soul in "Hades" to contact a soul in "Paradise"].

"Vettellini" later (op. cit., p. 290) stated that souls who are in the higher "Paradise" conditions usually find it difficult to communicate with mortals. Although those who are in "Hades" [="earthbound"] communicate easily, "They have no power to reach mortals if the latter do not lay themselves open to their influence by *attempting* to communicate" [i.e. by deliberately and persistently *"calling"* them].

On p. 314 of this book "Vettellini" said the same as "Judge Hatch", in the U.S.A.—that is, that, quite apart from help that may be given to *mortals* by the receipt of communications (providing assurance of survival, giving healing, issuing warnings, etc.), *it may help the discarnate communicators by providing an opportunity for service.* [Moreover, it "stimulates" them to renewed activities, doubtless by the "semi-physical" ectoplasmic emanations from the vehicle of vitality of the medium].

Dr Alice Gilbert (*Philip in the Spheres*, Aquarian Press,

1952, p. 56) was told by "Philip" of an instance in which she had "co-operated". A mother had lost contact with her boy during the war and was distracted. "Philip" said: "I realized it was a job for you. *Meanwhile I have taken Grandpa [from 'Paradise'] to her but she could only see him as a faint warm light. But you, being still on earth [and therefore with a vehicle of vitality], even though you were functioning in the astral plane [here='Paradise'], she could see, and you talked to her. When at last she grasped what had happened, you took her to her boy. ..."*

Cora L. V. Tappan, a woman who was reared in a small village and who had no education beyond the "three R's", received the following "communication": "The material world scoffs at the idea of bringing about anything by prayer. Intensity of thought in a given direction, if properly guided, may bring about almost anything; and that form of mental aspiration which *asks a certain favour* (if it be not in contravention of natural laws) will certainly bring about that favour, provided the guardian spirits can reach that thought, *the intensity of your thought* being sufficient to reach them. ... Prayer from sincere desire, expressed by many people for an object that is not in contravention of any law of the Divine Will, will surely affect a body of spirits who will surely bring about a desirable result. ..." (*Discourses*, J. Burns, 1875, p. 69.)

SUMMARY—*"Communicators" make the same statement as occurs in the Scriptures, i.e. that our prayers to God on behalf of others, including our enemies, may be answered via "ministrant spirits, sent out to serve".* (Heb. i, 14.)

REASON—"Communicators" go further than the Scriptures; they adduce an eminently reasonable explanation of their statement. *The total physical body of mortals includes the "semi-physical" vehicle of vitality, the "etheric body" of Theosophy, which constitutes a "bridge" or "link" between mortals and "angels" or "ministrant spirits" who inhabit relatively high "Paradise" conditions in the "super-physical" Soul Body. When we pray earnestly for other mortals, therefore, we may "co-operate" with the "angels" and do work that is difficult, if indeed possible, to them. The work is done especially during our periods of deep (dreamless) sleep. The knowledge of such possibilities enables us definitely to offer ourselves for such work before entering sleep and this facilitates "co-operation".*

2. "CO-OPERATION" THAT HELPS TO ESTABLISH A NEW WORLD ORDER

In *Journ. S.P.R.*, 40, 1960, pp. 276, 283, W. H. Salter pointed out that in the S.P.R. scripts that had been produced by Mrs Verrall, Mrs Holland, Miss Verrall [=Mrs Salter] and Mrs Willett, it was claimed that "a large number" of surviving souls, including the chief "communicators" of the scripts—Professor H. Sidgwick, F. W. H. Myers, Edmund Gurney, F. W. M. Balfour, Annie Marshall, Laura Lyttleton and Mary Catherine Lyttleton—were engaged in inaugurating "a new World Order based on international peace and social justice". Their work, which, the "communicators" stated, would be realized "within the not-too-distant future", in-volves the *"co-operation"* of a number of mortals (chiefly, of course, the psychics involved). Mr Salter dealt further with this matter in his book entitled *Zoar* (Sidgwick & Jackson, 1961, pp. 189, 204).

In an article in *Light* (LXXX, 1960, p. 161) the present writer dealt at length with this supposed plan of "co-operation", pointing out that numerous other "communicators" had been saying the same things for many years. The following is an example:

"W. F. Barrett" communicating to his wife, Lady Barrett (*Personality Survives Death*, Longmans, Green & Co. Ltd., 1937, p. 100) said that their "co-operation" for the benefit of humanity was in accordance with *"plans made for us on this side"*. He (p. 88) said that mortals should realize that the Soul has a Soul or "Etheric" Body through which comes the power of the Spirit, recharging the physical body with vitality. Those people who will become conscious of this Soul Body and its function as a bridge between Spirit and physical matter will avoid after-death residence in the "lower planes" [="Hades"]. He continued, "My great aim is now to show mortals the importance of developing the Soul or Etheric life *before* they leave the physical body." He stated: *"I hope to do that later through you—with you."*

"Barrett" was most urgent that he and his mortal wife should "co-operate" to make people realize that *"The spiritual life must be formed in the physical life*—that is the object for which God created the earth and the physical life thereon." As Jesus so often said by means of parables, earth-life is largely a "seed-time" and the immediate after-life a "harvest-time" (see *The Supreme Adventure*, James Clarke & Co., 1961, p. 235, by the present writer).

3. "CO-OPERATION" THAT HELPS THE DYING

"Deborah" asked her husband, W. S. Montgomery Smith, to concentrate his thoughts on a man who was dying. She told him to do this at night when the man would be *"quiet [because physically inactive] and receptive to power"* [*because the Soul Body is not "screened", "insulated" or "blinkered" by the physical body*]. She said, *"You are always in partnership with me. Our combined power acts as a mental cure. We can usually help both those who are ill and recover and those who are ill and pass over.* Their passing is easier through the healing power directed to them" (*Light in our Darkness*, Psychic Press Ltd., 1926, p. 43).

Here is a second example: "I had a young friend who was dying. One Saturday I awoke with all the sensations as if I were dying of haemorrhage. ... The next morning I saw the spirit-form of my friend. ... He looked happy and smiled at me. A day or two later I received a letter stating that he had passed away on the very Saturday. My spirit friends afterwards told me that, to give him the necessary spiritual strength for his upward flight, his spirit had been brought into my surroundings [which included the relatively loose vehicle of vitality] directly after his decease." (E. A. Tietkens, *Mediumistic and Psychical Experiences*, L.S.A. Ltd.)

The great seer Dr Rudolf Steiner made statements much like the following: "Christ set Himself to make a Path of Light straight from the World of Light [= 'Paradise'], through the dark blanket of fog in the astral plane [='Hades'], to the earth, so that spirits should be able to travel in freedom from this world to the next immune from the power of darkness. What all conscious spirits are trying to do is to make that Path into a Thoroughfare. Our loved ones on the other side are sending us material for our spirits to do our share in it. *They cannot do it all themselves, being no longer in the flesh, but they can show us how they are working, and can get us to co-operate.*" (Olive C. B. Pixley, *The Trail*, The C. W. Daniel Co., 1934.)

The "communicator" of Major T. W. Pole (*Private Dowding*, Watkins, 1917, p. 75) spoke of "the mists which hang over the great River [='Hades'] separating your world [=earth] from ours [='Paradise']". He pointed out that "all souls must pass through these 'mists' [which are in the earth-belt corresponding to the vehicle of vitality of men's bodies] on leaving their physical form for the last time". In these between-regions are unpleasant conditions that have been "created by discordant human thinking". Discarnate souls who are in "Paradise" conditions work to destroy them. He then spoke of "co-operation" as follows: *"Many still in the flesh are called upon to work there with us during both waking and sleeping hours."* Like "Barrett" and Lord Dowding, he added, *"I want to impress upon you the importance of such work "*

This "communicator" ("Private Dowding") made a statement identical to that of "Stead": after saying that "negative" methods of communicating (e.g. automatic writing and trance mediumship) may involve dangers to the medium, whereas the "positive" method (i.e. natural and normal clairvoyance, without the loss of consciousness) is safe, he said, *"The veil can also be safely lifted during sleep."*

Major Pole (op. cit., 1917, p. 98), who was present at the death of "Major P.", described what he saw (with clairvoyant vision). He emphasized the fact that *"Prayer and protecting thought are invaluable at such a time."*

H. M. Nathan's "communicators" (*Man's Cosmic Horizon*, Rider & Co. Ltd.) told him the following: "Thoughts vibrate down the ether and accumulate through the ages; evil ones, of low vibration, collect like clouds; they fog the mental atmosphere [in 'Hades'] until dispelled by shafts of good thoughts. *Human thought is infinitely more able to dispel such clouds than is spirit-thought, being of a more equivalent wave-length [on account of the vehicle of vitality]."*

SUMMARY—*The "co-operation", which includes the prayers of mortals (and especially of those that are more or less psychic*

—a condition of which they may be unaware), can help those of the dying who experience some difficulty in (a) *fully releasing the vehicle of vitality from the physical body or* (b) *in getting away from earth-conditions after it has been fully released. Thereafter "co-operation" can help in the passage through the "Hades" region which lies between earth and "Paradise".*

REASON—*When a man dies, the total body that is released consists of the "super-physical" Soul Body plus the "semi-physical" vehicle of vitality. The latter constitutes a link or a bridge and every newly-dead man is "psychic" by virtue of this bodily constitution: he is particularly susceptible to any helpful thoughts and feelings from mortals. The latter possess a vehicle of vitality and are (in a bodily sense, and therefore effectively) "nearer" to the newly-dead man than are the "angels" in "Paradise" conditions. (He will enter "Paradise" a little later—after the vehicle of vitality has been shed).*

4. "CO-OPERATION" THAT HELPS THE NEWLY-DEAD

In America, "Judge Hatch" told Elsa Barker (*War Letters from the Living Dead Man*, Rider, 1915, p. 120), "There are many non-combatants in all lands whose hours of sleep are given to a devoted labour for the souls that need help so horribly." Again (op. cit., p. 235) he urged her not to waste strength and gave this reason: "If we use you sometimes as a material base on which to plant our etheric feet for a greater spring into space, remember that you offered yourself for the service of the world." Still again (op. cit., p. 253): "I, to whom you look for strength, find also strength in you [who have a vehicle of vitality]. You are a solid platform from which I can spring when I need the [ectoplasmic] force of a material base."

In England, the "communicator" of G. Trevor (*Death's Door Opens*, 1950, p. 30) told him of his work in helping men who had "just passed over" (i.e. in acting as a "deliverer") and said that Trevor had sometimes assisted in this work during his hours of sleep. This "communicator" also said that Trevor helped his two mortal brothers with his thoughts and prayers (op. cit., p. 37).

The (discarnate) husband of "M.L.S." (*A Guide Book to the Land of Peace*, John Wadsworth, p. 16) said that the dying and the newly-dead should pray: *"If they do not pray for help, we cannot find them. If they call for help, the prayer makes a sort of path upon which we can find them."*

"Joyce", the deceased daughter of Mrs G. Vivian, B.A. (*Love Conquers Death*, L.S. Publications, p. 61) similarly told her that she was being "trained" to "co-operate" in helping the newly-dead. Later (op. cit., p. 68) "Joyce" answered a question as to the nature of her own work as follows: "Amongst other things, helping to train young children who have come over early to this world. We don't let them feel the loss of their mothers: I bring them home to you, Mummie, and in the garden to play, so that they can gain earth-experience."

Mabel Beatty (*The Temple of the Body*, Rider, 1930, p. 72) was also told that the recently-dead who are "in a grey mist of ignorance" are helped not only by discarnate souls but also sometimes by mortals.

Mrs Kelway Bamber's discarnate son (*Claude's Book*, Psychic Book Club, 1918, p. 49) "communicated" as follows: "When your body sleeps, your soul comes over here and we spend hours together. ... Thousands of people come over in this way every night, and are more awake while here than on earth in their mortal bodies. To do this, people must be spiritually evolved to a certain degree. ... Sometimes we work amongst those who have just awakened in the spirit world and are bewildered. ... We explain to them where they are and bring their friends to see them.

"*It seems curious to you that you should be able to do this even better than I, as you are still in a mortal body; but that is the very reason. You see, you* [*possessing a vehicle of vitality*] *are the 'half-way house', as it were,* for along that little cord that connects your Soul [Body] and [physical] body are travelling thoughts and desires of earth. You are therefore more in touch with the earth and so feel more familiar to one who has just come over. You are still controlled and limited by your earth-body while connected with it."

Kamatini (*The Soul's Journeys*, Rider) mentioned a man who died but who, for many days, could not get free from the physical body and "earth-conditions" [i.e. he was still enmeshed in the vehicle of vitality or "body-veil"]. "And all the time," said the "communicator", "those patient helpers did not leave him for one moment. *They knew the only way to free that particular soul, and to break down the strong ties that bound it to the earth, was the earnest prayer of one still in the flesh*" [*and therefore possessing the vehicle of vitality*].

A communicator "Friend H!!!" (*The Dead—Active*, Fernie, 1919, p. 21) mentioned his work as a "deliverer", i.e. in helping the newly-dead. He added, "You can help us in this missionary work. I am referring to the help you may give (and many of you, *especially the psychic ones*, do) if you are sufficiently sensitive to spirit power to be withdrawn from your bodies during sleep for a sufficient time to go about with us, *helping us to rouse the lethargic ones.* ... *The more you cultivate your spirit-gifts on earth, the more useful you are now* [=*during sleep, etc.*]. This is in addition to the untold help it will be to each one of you having had insight into the work while your spirits still inhabit the flesh."

A later "communication" (op. cit., p. 119) bears on the above. It was said that discarnate "deliverers" attend battles and aid the dying—that they "deliver the spirit from its prison-house of the flesh". These "deliverers" consist of "those who have *recently* left the body" [=still possess the vehicle of vitality] and who therefore find it "much easier" to get close to the earth. Having done their work, they pass the newly-born soul to *others* [who have shed the vehicle of vitality and entered "Paradise" conditions]. The latter, who were unable to get "close to the earth", complete the process.

Constance Wiley (*A Star of Hope*, The C. W. Daniel Co. Ltd., 1938, p. 56) was told: "During your hours of sleep you were working in our world, and did much to help the cause of the mission on which, with others, you were sent; it was a mission of importance to some who had been projected *very suddenly* into our world. You have a very convincing way which helps especially *because you are still in the flesh* [=*with a vehicle of vitality*]. Though this may seem strange to you. It is so. They have, you see, so recently been in the flesh and had no preparation or thought of 'passing', that they cannot realize death has taken place. ... Then it is that people like yourself, *who desire to serve*, are of great help in convincing them that they have 'passed on', and help them to understand and listen to those who are sent [from 'Paradise' conditions] to be their teachers. ... *Tell all you can that they work for others in this way during their earth-lives, if they truly desire to serve and pray to God to permit them to do so.*"

Again (op. cit., p. 75), "I ask your prayers for many who have suffered in the East in the floods and earthquakes. Many of them are not able to realize where they are or how they got there. Their 'passing' was so *sudden* and they were in health, they had no illness, therefore it was to them more difficult to realize their 'passing'. ... *They must be taught to be up and doing and learn how to pray for help, and be ready and willing to be taught how to serve. You can help in this work by prayer and in your sleep-life. I come for your help to do this.*"

"Barrett", communicating to Lady Barrett, a medical woman (*Personality Survives Death*, Longmans, Green & Co. Ltd., 1937, p. 113), mentioned a welfare-worker who had died when over-strained. He told Lady Barrett: "I don't think you have any idea of the extent to which your thoughts helped her." He pointed out: "*We are extra sensitive to the thoughts of mortals, especially in the early days [while still retaining the vehicle of vitality], when our minds hover between the earth we have left and the new land on which our feet are not yet firmly planted [= 'Paradise']. In that between condition [='Hades'] we need ... constructive, helpful, loving thoughts.*"

An identical "communication" was given by the newly-dead "Wilberforce" (*Letters from the Other Side*, Watkins, 1919, p. 2). He stated: "Here, in the border-land [='Hades'] we can be easier helped and hurt than when protected [='insulated', 'blanketed' or 'screened'] by the physical body." *During this brief after-death period he was still "united with the physical forces" [=vehicle of vitality]. But later [when the vehicle of vitality was shed and he had entered "Paradise" in the Soul Body], he could not contact mortals unless and until, by their loving thoughts, they provided a "ladder".*

"Wilberforce" (op. cit., 1919, p. 14) gave an example of "co-operation" in helping the newly-dead. "E. L." was "mentally obscured", since he was "still cast-iron-bound in prejudice". Asked how he was aware of this

condition of the discarnate "E.L.", "Wilberforce" replied that it was through the "co-operation" of the
incarnate psychic. The latter had sent "thoughts of
sympathy" to "E.L." and these acted "like tapers in
the dark" to "Wilberforce", leading him to "E.L."
Again (p. 79) "Wilberforce said, *"Prayer rings up the
legions of unseen helpers and guardians. ..."* Still later
(p. 138) he explained the process as follows. "To us,
the material world is practically *non est.* The *soul of* your
world [='Paradise'] is sensible to us—we perceive
your thoughts and sentiments as emanations. The *facts*
of your world [=physical objects and events] do not
reach us unless you send out to the Supreme, or to one
of us, *a cry, an entreaty for guidance. That is the rationale of
prayer to some extent."*

Later (op. cit., p. 127) "Wilberforce" said that he
left "Paradise" (his "home") and re-entered the
"borderland realm" [="Hades"] in order to help the
newly-dead. He repeated his former statement that the
transition from earth to "Hades" makes a great differ-
ence since the Soul Body is no longer shielded by the
physical body (which "acts as a *buffer*"). Hence, he said,
in "Hades", "the conflict with evil is, in some senses,
intensified".

"Stead" (*The Blue Island*, Experiences of a New
Arrival Beyond the Veil, Hutchinson, 1922, p. 94),
during his short after-death period in "Hades", communicated identical ideas: *"In this land ['Hades'] we
are much more sensitive than whilst on earth, and when
thoughts are directed to us by mortals we have a direct call from
those currents of thought thus generated. We are practically
always able to come in close contact with the person who is
thinking of us.* When near and acclimatized to his conditions, we can impress thoughts and ideas upon his
mind. *He will think they are his own normal thoughts."*

Geoffrey Hodson (*The Science of Seership*, Rider & Co. Ltd., p. 130) was told: "It is not necessary for those who greet the new arrival in the next world to be dead—frequently they are still living on earth."

"Miss Thomas" (deceased) (Revd. C. Drayton Thomas, *The Life Beyond Death with Evidence*, W. Collins & Co. Ltd., 1928) described the emanation that is essential for trance-communication. She said, "It is a no-man's land between the two conditions, yours [*physical*] and ours ['Paradise']. *It is supposed that communication concerns earth-people [in the physical body] and spirit-people [in the Soul Body] whereas there is also the peculiar bridgeway which has to be used, and which is neither one nor the other, but has some of the characteristics of each [=the vehicle of vitality*]. Medium and sitter are, in part, working in a condition which is not entirely yours, and we work in one which is not entirely ours. *It is a pooling of resources which creates the bridge. It is on the borderline between matter and spirit*." "Mr Thomas" (the deceased father of Drayton Thomas) said, "Our vibrations [in 'Paradise'] are not operative by themselves on your plane [=earth]. When we do something on your plane (which is not our plane), we have to make use of that in you which corresponds most nearly to ours, but which is not ours." The Revd. C. Drayton Thomas commented on these statements thus: "Between the body and the Self there would be recognized *an intermediary* [=*vehicle of vitality*] which translates sense-vibrations on the brain into perceptions by the Self."

"Miss Thomas" said that she could "co-operate" with her (incarnate) brother since his thoughts "provided a kind of lead" which she followed—that it was as if he "laid a trail" with his thoughts and she followed it (as one would follow scraps of paper laid for the purpose), eventually helping those about whom her brother was concerned. In this way, she said, discarnates were able to accomplish what might otherwise be impossible. This "communicator" also said that the newly-dead are able to help children who have "passed over" because there is only a small vibrational "gulf" between them. She further said (*Beyond Life's Sunset*, Psychic Press Ltd.) that she herself tended some newly-dead infants—since she herself was newly-dead *"there was something familiar about her which comforted the little strangers"*.

A "communicator" told Olive C. B. Pixley (*Listening In*, L.S.A. Publications Ltd.: "I never knew what prayer was until I came here. It is *the* force that operates in my world, as electricity does in yours. *Prayer materially alters our conditions. When you pray for those who have passed on it is like giving them presents: you alter conditions that can be changed only by the force of prayer."*

The discarnate "Heslop" (*Speaking Across the Border-line*, Charles Taylor, 1912, p. 11) thanked his incarnate wife for her prayers on his behalf. He said, "We need your prayers here, just as we needed them on earth. ... It is one of the saddest mistakes, amongst many that have encrusted themselves round with the religious teaching of modern times, that, when we die, the tie is practically severed with those on earth, and that the loved ones left behind have no longer any power to help those who have 'gone on before'."

In his later "communications" (*Further Messages Across the Border-line*, Charles Taylor, 1921, p. 67), "Heslop", like so many others, told his incarnate wife that during sleep her Soul [in the Soul Body] "gladly" floated away from her physical body and the physical world, along with "ministering spirits" [="deliverers"] into "one of the beautiful spheres of light and love" [="Paradise"]. He informed her: "As psychic development proceeds, you become *conscious of* [*='remember'*] these journeys, and the memory of what you have seen and heard is a priceless possession, a fore-taste of the glory of the life-to-come." He added, "But it is not always wise for these spirit-journeys to be too well remembered—the contrast would make life unendur-able, so in mercy it is often veiled from your minds.

"When times of great stress come, as in the present war, *we call upon you to help us in our work for those newly-passed to this side. And you come in the night and aid us greatly while your physical frames are asleep. ... When any of you are willing to help us, we greatly value it.*"

SUMMARY—*While we are in the physical body, it acts as a "screen", an "insulator" or a "buffer" and we are seldom, if ever, directly aware of the thoughts and feelings of others. The newly-dead, having shed this "insulation", are directly affected by the thoughts and feelings and emotions of mortals (i.e. they are telepathic): hence mortals of good-will can aid the newly-dead by prayers on their behalf and by constructive, encouraging thoughts.*

Those who have suffered sudden and unexpected death (in-cluding men killed in battle) may be particularly bewildered and therefore in need of help.

REASON—*The "body" of the newly-dead includes not only the "super-physical" Soul Body, but also the "semi-physical" vehicle of vitality: the latter is a link or bridge between the Soul Body (the instrument of thought, emotion and will) and the physical body (the instrument of physical action). Hence, as long as the newly-dead retain the vehicle of vitality, they are readily affected by the thoughts and feelings of mortals (who, like them, possess a vehicle of vitality), whereas "angels" in "Paradise" conditions (who no longer possess that "bridge")', find it difficult to impress and help them. Mortals who have a positive desire to be of service, and who pray to God to be*

*allowed to serve (especially if they are more or less psychic—
a condition of which they may be unaware), can "co-operate"
with "angels" and thus render invaluable aid to the newly-
dead.*

5. "CO-OPERATION" THAT HELPS THE
"EARTHBOUND"
(the "spirits in prison" of the Scriptures)

Lord Dowding (*Lychgate*, Rider, 1945) mentioned the
work which mortals do during sleep. He (p. 13) cited a
"communicator" (Clarice) as saying that many people
are unable to undertake such for lack of training—
during sleep their Soul Bodies do not get far from (but
lie "exactly above") their physical bodies. He gave the
same explanation as many others of the value of mortals
in "co-operation": *the "earthly vibrations" of mortals [from
the vehicle of vitality] are "necessary to complete the full
quota of radiation which is required by God's Agents* [=dis-
carnate souls in 'Paradise' conditions and therefore in
the Soul Body] when they are working on earth or among
those inhabiting the lower places close to earth [=
'Hades]." Lord Dowding admitted, "I am too ignorant
to be able to tell you why this should be so, but I know
it to be a fact." But he was sure that "It permits us to
participate in the work of God's angels." He insisted
that the dead need the loving thoughts and prayers of
mortals.

On p. 50 Lord Dowding referred to "rescue circles"
(in which "earthbound" souls, delayed in "Hades"
conditions, are helped). He again said that he did not
know why the help of mortals was necessary—"I only
know that *there is some quality in our human earthly vibrations,* if they be of *love,* which is needed to complete the
great Spiral of God's power when it is used in the astral
region close to the earth [=in 'Hades']."

Lord Dowding (op. cit., p. 26) then referred to what might be described as "co-operation" *in reverse.* A "communicator" who was "earthbound" said that the fact that he was allowed to use a medium's body to do "automatic writing" enabled him to "gather power of this type from the earth-plane" and that with this power he could influence mortals in the right direction.

Lord Dowding was also (op. cit., p. 60) told that suitable mortals during sleep meet those who are suffering sudden death (e.g. in battle) and help them (i.e. some mortals, as well as some discarnate souls, can act as "deliverers").

In a later book (*The Dark Star*, Museum Press Ltd., 1951, p. 68) *Dowding again emphasized the fact that mortals can help the "earthbound" to move out of "Hades" into "Paradise" conditions. He, we believe rightly, regarded the ignorance and neglect of this matter as "the chief failing of all the main religions of the world."* He (op. cit., p. 69) cited a "communicator" as saying, "You say, 'Why do not we [who are in "Paradise" conditions] do it all? Why should we turn to you [mortals] for help?'" and as answering, "*There are many cases which we can deal with, but there are others whom we cannot reach except through the minds of earth-people.*"

Several references to "co-operation" were made in Dr Alice Gilbert's book *Philip in the Spheres* (Aquarian Press, 1952). On p. 17 she asked her discarnate son, "Philip", as follows: "What does 'earthbound' mean? I've read *Lychgate*, by Lord Dowding, about circles held to help the earthbound [=in 'Hades']. Why can't these people contact those in your [='Paradise'] world? Why must they be helped by people here [=mortals] to contact you [souls in 'Paradise']?" "Philip" replied that the "earthbound" are "neither in one world or another" [=neither in the physical world nor in

"Paradise"]. He said, "It is one of the hardest jobs, from outside, to penetrate into the shell-image of an 'earthbound' person. But if a *psychically sensitive* person of *helpful nature* can get through to them the knowledge of a further state (to which a mere act of will may open the door), then usually they begin to emerge." "Philip" added that, while some who are "earthbound" have *fixed ideas* [i.e. are "earthbound" in a *mental* sense] others "are still on earth in its etheric form" [=in the "Hades" belt because retaining the vehicle of vitality— i.e. "earthbound" in a *bodily* sense].

In America "The Revd. T. Scott" communicating to Dr J. M. Peebles (*Immortality*, Colby & Rich, 1883, p. 148) stated: "There are dark, mirthful, and malicious spirits [='earthbound'] in the lower spheres [= 'Hades']. It is part of the employment of the higher to teach and uplift the lower. But it is not all spirits that can descend to these spheres—hence, many come within the atmosphere of earth and within the influence of communicating circles ['rescue circles' of mortals]. *Well-disposed mortals form a bond of connection through which the lower intelligences receive instruction from the higher.*"

The "communicator" of Wilfred Brandon (*Open the Door!*, Alfred A. Knopf, 1935, p. xviii) stated, "We are only too glad to be of service, but we are frequently forced to abandon our work for the *lack of power to communicate.* We hope that those people who also can hear, or see, or write automatically [=who are *psychic*] will *call upon us in their thoughts and prepare to do their part in the co-operation of the two planes of being that are really only two sides of the same thing—human experience.*"

Again, speaking of men killed in battle (op. cit., p. 97) he said, "Individual thoughts and prayers, strongly projected, with concentration and *the name of the beloved dead spoken*, often reach their object and still, for a time, the tormented mind. ... *We here do all we can, but we need help.* We ask it here, prayer—and by prayer we mean instructive, helpful thought, directed to a soul—will aid us in our task." Brandon's "communicator" (op. cit., p. 137) also said, "Drug-fiends are possible obsessors after death; also alcoholics and sexualists. Sometimes revenge is a motive. ... The restoring of such obsessed mortals is but one phase of the possible benefits of co-operation with us."

One "communicator" told the American lawyer E. C. Randall (*The Dead have Never Died*, Geo. Allen & Unwin Ltd., 1918, p. 65) that *the "earthbound" are, as yet, "living so much on the earth-plane that you mortals can secure and hold their attention more closely than we can."*

In a later book (*Frontiers of the After-Life*, Alfred A. Knopf, 1922) Randall (p. 46) cited the following "communication" : "It is almost impossible for us [in 'Paradise'] to help some spirits [in 'Hades'], as they have no desire to be better. *Prayer by those still on earth is the only thing which can help them.*"

Randall summed up his own observations (op. cit., p. 154) as follows: "Those who are advanced [=in 'Paradise'] in the after-life are ever anxious to help those below and they do a wonderful work. *But there are many whom they cannot reach, and it is only by blending their forces with ours [who have vehicles of vitality] that a condition was created where these poor souls could be brought to a realization of this condition. ... Spirit people are limited in their sphere as we are in ours and so, for twenty-two years, we worked together to help 'earthbound' spirits. It was the most important work I ever did.*" This remarkable declaration, made by an eminent American lawyer, accords with that of the eminent British soldier, Lord Dowding.

In South Africa one "communicator" told F. W.

Fitzsimons (*Opening the Psychic Door*, Hutchinson, 1933) that, though he himself was invisible to the "earthbound", Fitzsimons *"from a physical body [which included the vehicle of vitality] would be denser and would be seen as a solid person."* Another said that, *while he was within the "magnetic aura" [=the aggregate vehicle of vitality] produced at the seance, he could see and address (and consequently help) the "earthbound": under other conditions, he was invisible and intangible to them.*

The discarnate "Wilberforce" (*Letters from the Other Side*, 1919, p. 44) said that "darkened ones" (=the "earthbound") "often get no help except through the incarnate". The reason for this was that they are "in closer touch" with mortals than with "the disembodied". He added that, while people should respond to requests for prayers by the "earthbound", "few are fit to undertake this work, and should not seek it [via 'rescue circles'] of their own volition". He insisted, "To sit deliberately and invite that kind of visitant seems to me folly."

Again, "Wilberforce" (op. cit., p. 60) said, *"Assuredly souls still in and out of the body, consciously or unconsciously, unite in all dynamic spiritual effort—else were your prayers shorn of much of their power, their efficacy to bring about results. God works through His ministers, in and out of the body."*

Doris and Hilary Severn (*In the Next Room*, Constable & Co. Ltd., 1911, p. 29) asked an "earthbound" "communicator", "Why come to us? Why not ask the angels?" The answer was: *"Where are the angels? We have not seen any! You [mortals who are psychic] are nearer to us."*

Conan Doyle (*Light*, LXV, 1925, p. 86) pointed out that certain discarnate Red Indians (many of whom are regarded as teachers) "were not to teach but to be

taught" by the mortal psychics. He compared their
condition to that of the "earthbound" souls at "rescue
circles" and asked a "communicator" why "the higher
spirits" fail to do the necessary work. He was told:
"*These* ['*earthbound*'] *people are very much nearer to you than
to us. You can reach them where we fail.*"

A communicator of "Friend H!!!" (*The Dead—Active*,
Fernie, 1919, p. 21) said, "Never mind *whether you
remember* where you have been, or what work you have
been doing, when you return to your waking consciousness [=re-enter the physical body]: the work has been
done and *you, while attached to the physical body, can often
give far more help and comfort to those in the dark states* [=
'*earthbound*'] *than we can.* ... *There is that certain something
of earth belonging to you* [=*the vehicle of vitality*], *which is
of the utmost value to us in this work. We are thankful for your
co-operation, even if unknown to you. You little know how often
we* [*who have no vehicle of vitality*] *take French leave of you
people on earth who can be made use of for this purpose.*"

Margaret Eyre (*The Revealing Light*, Vincent Stuart,
1962, pp. 19–20) was told "There is work waiting to be
done. ... It concerns the welfare of persons who have
left life as you know it, and are not yet ready for the life
here [in 'Paradise']. Their need is very great. My
companion has a scheme, but it is incomplete without
co-operation from you. It consists in interesting these
people ... in those about them and so awakening them
to progress. ... To create this interest, she brings before
them, in turn, *thoughts of someone or something each has
loved. Quickly—before this dies away—she indicates to each
some small movement which might be made in result, a wish,
in prayer, a kind word, a happy thought. On the vibrations of
these, she can bring to those who cause them similar values from
elsewhere, thus multiplying the result many times.* This, in
cumulative effect, works wonders on these poor sufferers,

for they do suffer in their *hopeless negative inactivity.* You wonder where you come in? *We want you to direct your love to these, her charges, and to claim, as you do so, fruition of God, wherever it touches them. They, poor souls, need the earth vibrations as well as those that we send [from 'Paradise'] for they are not yet fully of us, whereas you, as still an earth-inhabitant [and possessing a vehicle of vitality] have supplies of the very thing they need and which we seek for them."*

Again (op. cit., p. 64) "Your first teacher could not have carried out his work in the dark lands [='Hades'] without your love, because owing to his own progress, *he lacks some of the essential materials; these you supply [from the vehicle of vitality]. By your emotional power ... you have a wealth and reserve of comfort ...* upon which, on their behalf, he can draw at will." Still again (op. cit., p. 89) "Your first teacher wishes you to know about the work you do with him, principally at night, when you are taken to those outlands [='Hades'] where his re-deeming work is carried on. *You make contact with those to whom you are sent and find means whereby they will them-selves move, however slightly, towards the light.* ... For this purpose your help is invaluable because you are now able to pour forth a flood of warmth, and so stimulation —it is warmth, comfort, friendliness and hope that they crave. As response is made, wistful, blind, selfish, but response—your teacher is able to place into this opening a seed of life, a thought, a desire, a memory, even a pain, which will draw on the one who feels it. You are sent with him because you are being trained to face torture, despair, filth, etc., the only condition in which such work can be done."

P. E. Cornillier (*The Survival of the Soul,* Kegan Paul, Trench, Trubner & Co. Ltd., 1921) gave several French instances in which "earthbound" "communicators", through the entranced medium, Reine, requested the "co-operation" of mortals. On p. 18 "Henri Morin" pleaded "Pray for me!" On p. 113 a woman used the same words. This request was made by "earthbound" souls in Germany to Frau Hauffe (who was "more than half dead").

The discarnate father of Cornillier (op. cit., 1921) (who was in the "lower spheres", i.e. "earthbound" in "Hades"), "co-operated" in order that Cornillier could contact "Aunt Susan". (Although the latter had been a "good" woman in the moral sense, she had *fixed ideas on religion* which kept her mentally "earthbound". When told the truth she could not accept it and thought it came from the "devil"). In this case one "earthbound" spirit co-operated with mortals to aid another "earthbound" soul.

Although we are told that special arrangements are made for those who have given their lives for others, suicides are necessarily "earthbound" at first: the condition is partly that of mental origin (the refusal of life) and partly bodily (the retention of the vehicle of vitality). "Kit", communicating to his mother (*My Son Kit*, Psychic Press Ltd., 1947, p. 55) said he was working among suicides. She said, "*Mortals* can help in such cases with prayers and healing thoughts." A "communicator" (*Journ.* S.P.R., 1908) who had committed suicide and was "suffering" pleaded for "*earthly* prayers."

One of J. Arthur Findlay's communicators (*The Edge of the Etheric*, Rider, 1931) acknowledged help he had received from still-embodied friends. He said, "I thank you for the comfort you gave me since I came to this side of life. *I went out in darkness but was brought back to the light through the instrumentality of the friends I met in your surroundings.*" Another said, "God bless you all for every word and thought which you sent out to me during my stubborn time after passing."

Mr Findlay (*The Rock of Truth*, Rider & Co. Ltd.) also said, "It is not these people who haunt the earth [the 'earthbound'] who *come* to seances, but they are sometimes *brought* for the purpose of awakening them to a realization of their new surroundings. Such seances are called 'Rescue Circles'. They are for the purpose of awakening an urge for something better in those people who have never been able to untie their minds from earth, and reach the surface of their new abode. *The old term 'Hades' doubtless was meant for this hinterland between the two surfaces, where roam undeveloped souls. Etheric [='Paradise'] missionaries, however, are always at work, trying to enlighten them and raise them by thought to their proper plane, and, with the desire for something better, they leave our earth's surface [='Hades'] and reach the one above [='Paradise'] quite naturally. These helpers often find this impossible to do and make use of us on earth to help them, as we are able to influence those backward people in a way they cannot do.*"

The "communicator" of Montgomery Smith (op. cit., p. 64) mentioned suicides who were on "lower planes" of the after-life and pointed out: "Only two lots of people can help on these lower planes, namely people from earth and very good people who have passed over—not the average person. The Etheric [=Soul] Body is too sensitive and [in average people] not sufficiently under control. A *mortal* is more protected by the link with the physical, and the fact that he must quickly return there. If a *discarnate* spirit placed himself at a disadvantage on a 'low plane', he would have no armour to call him back—he would be all there. A mortal would be called back at the least sign of danger: he can pay occasional visits."

Later (op. cit.), he mentioned a girl who, after "rather a tragic life", had died. He pleaded: "Send out thoughts and pray for her. *Your thoughts can help such people more than we can.*"

Mr Hoey (*Truths from the Spirit World*, Hoey, 1907, p. 40) was told that mortals can help a discarnate soul on the "astral plane" [here=in "Hades" conditions] "by *loving thoughts and prayers on his behalf*". Later (op. cit., p. 105) he said, "There are souls who need the prayers of those on earth, even as they need the aid of those behind the veil [=in 'Paradise' conditions]—not *bad*, but rather *materialistic* souls. ..." Still later (p. 122) Hoey was urged not to reproach himself for being (as he thought) unable to do psychic work, i.e. clairvoyance, etc. The "communicator" said, "*In your sleep, maybe, you are doing far better work in your Astral* [=*soul*] *Body, since the desire was in you.*" He admitted, "Few are permitted to know of their work during sleep, though we know."

Mrs Annie Brittain ('*Twixt Earth and Heaven*, Rider, 1935, p. 86) was told: "You have been used as an instrument by the more evolved spirits [in 'Paradise'] to show them [the 'earthbound' in a 'misty sphere', i.e. 'Hades'] the light." She was given the same reason for this facility as were so many others. "*Coming from the earth-plane, and bringing with you a spirit-nature`nearer to the physical than ours, we have been able to use you to link up a chain from the higher to the lower.*"

The discarnate "Heslop" (*Further Messages Across the Border-line*, Charles Taylor, 1921, p. 28) said to his incarnate wife, "You ask me, 'What becomes, after death, of those who lead idle and careless lives?' God has many ways on this side in which the lessons of gentleness, calmness, patience, love, forgiveness, fortitude, etc., which should have been learned on earth are taught and acquired here, but one thing is certain—they *have* to be learned either on earth or here ... Another thing is certain—it is far easier to acquire this knowledge in the earth surroundings than on this side. ... It is for this reason that many ('earthbound') disembodied spirits return, in their spirit-bodies, to earth, striving to gain from *earthly teachers* what they failed to learn when with you. The distress of these poor souls, when they awaken here and find what their lives have really been! It is heartrending!"

Later (op. cit., p. 53) "Heslop" returned to this theme. "You on earth have power to help and bless, and to awaken and teach those who have left the earth and are wandering in ignorance on the Border-line [='Hades', between earth and 'Paradise']. He (p. 73) continued as follows: "Numbers of discarnate spirits return to your world to acquire from *earthly teachers* what they failed to learn in earth-life. Now this is a fact of the greatest importance. *It means that the influence of mortals, in thought, word and deed, affects for good or evil, spirit-people who are invisible to them.* ... *The more earnest of them throng your churches, chapels and lecture-halls, to receive help and teaching there.* ... Intellectual religion does not help you at all. It serves a purpose in convincing a certain class of mind of the truth [of survival], but, unless one so convinced goes on to practise, by unselfish love, the truths he has acquired intellectually, it pro- fiteth nothing. Love is the foundation ... of all religion. ... Prayer and love are the most potent influences with heaven to bring down spiritual gifts to men. *No man prays alone.*"

A newly-dead "communicator" of A. Farnese (*A Wanderer in the Spirit Lands*, W. J. Sinkins, 1896, p. 25) was told: "*For good or evil, your desires are prayers and call around you powers to answer them for you.*"

Fr. J. Greber, a Roman Catholic priest of twenty-five years' standing, who knew nothing of psychical re- search, etc., and who investigated by using an ignorant

German farm-boy, published his results in a book entitled *Communication with the Spirit World* (Felsberg, 1932). On p. 112 of this work he recorded a "communication" to the effect that discarnate souls who temporarily possessed the bodies of mediums should be tested as to their status and motives. If they should prove to be "suffering" [in "Hades"] "but well-disposed", i.e. not definitely evil, he should "pray with them". The "communicator" added, "In this way you will be doing a great kindness. They will be grateful to you for it ever after."

The "communicator" of *I Awoke* (David Stott, 1895, p. 36) spoke of the "earthbound", "souls in prison", who "could not tear themselves away from their former [earth] surroundings" and told his psychic: "*they are sometimes helped by counsel from your side*". He said that most "revanents", i.e. "ghosts", discarnate souls who can occasionally be seen and heard by non-psychics [because they still retain the "semi-physical" vehicle of vitality] are of the "earthbound" type. He (p. 39) further gave his own experience as follows: "Between my death to the old and the resurrection to the new [=between shedding the physical body and becoming fully conscious, of 'Paradise' conditions, in the Soul Body, i.e. while the vehicle of vitality was still unshed]" he had "visited" the "earthbound" in "Hades" and had been able to set one of them free. The man had acknowledged that he had been wrong and he then passed through the "second death" [=shed the vehicle of vitality, a process that normally occurs about three days after physical death] and entered "a new earth and a new heaven" [="Paradise" conditions].

SUMMARY—*The "communicators" state that mortals (especially those who are more or less psychic—a condition of which they may be unaware), during periods of deep sleep, may "co-operate" with discarnate souls who are in "Paradise" conditions to aid discarnate souls who are "earthbound" in "Hades" conditions. The latter may be delayed, either because of mental factors (fixed ideas, sensuality, etc.), or bodily considerations (the fact that they still have to shed the vehicle of vitality from the total after-death "double"). Those mortals who have overcome self and are therefore free from sensuality, jealousy, criticism, self-righteousness, etc., are most useful in such work, since the conditions contacted are sometimes those of a moral slum; many shrink from them. The loving and helpful thoughts and the prayers of mortals help the "earthbound" considerably. There must be a positive desire to help and to understand.*

REASON—*The "co-operation" of mortals for the benefit of the "earthbound" (including suicides) is desirable because mortals still possess the "semi-physical" vehicle of vitality (variously described as "earthly vibrations" and "something of the earth"). On this account mortals, and especially those who are more or less psychic (=with "loose" vehicles of vitality) are near the "earthbound" (who have retained—whereas they should normally have shed—the vehicle of vitality). "Ministrant angels" in "Paradise" conditions (whose vehicle of vitality has been shed at the "second death") are at a disadvantage in this respect. Thus mortals who are definitely well-disposed, by their prayers and kind thoughts, can lift "earthbound" souls into slightly higher conditions in which they are accessible to "ministering angels". In the absence of this mortal help, much angel-ministration must be delayed.*

6. "CO-OPERATION" THAT HELPS COMMUNICATION

"Barrett" told Lady Barrett (*Personality Survives Death*, Longmans, Green & Co. Ltd., 1937, p. 170) that communication should not be "*an end in itself*". He considered: "The important part is not the *communication* ... but *the preparing oneself for that other life*—that is what I want to help people to do through you." He regarded communication itself as "a matter of secondary importance" and said, "It is not even advisable for everybody at their present stage of development."

Later (op. cit., p. 186) "Barrett" stated: "It is not always right for mortals to communicate with us; people are not always *spiritually ready—many may be psychic, but if not spiritually ready to use the power, they often hurt themselves and others.*"

"Judge Hatch", communicating to Elsa Barker (*Letters from a Living Dead Man*, Rider & Co. Ltd., 1914, pp. 22, 243, 286) made various statements that indicated "co-operation" to communicate. The action was sometimes described as passing from the "living" (psychics) to the "dead" and sometimes as vice versa. An example of the former was in connection with "Hatch's" failure to "find" (i.e. to contact) a mortal friend. He suggested, "Perhaps it is necessary for you [i.e. incarnates, who possess the vehicle of vitality] to think strongly of us [discarnates] to make the way easiest." Many other "communicators" make this claim. For example, "Lancelot" (*Letters from Lancelot*, Dunstan, 1931, p. 74) said, "I can go whenever Granny is thinking of me and talk to her spirit." An example of what might be called a statement as to "two-way traffic" in emotion, as between the "living" and the "dead", is the following: "When man is excited, exalted or in any way intensified in his *emotional* life, the spirits draw near to him. That is the secret of inspiration; that is why anger grows with what it feeds on ... hateful spirits ... enjoy the excitement of anger in others. ..."

Again, "Hatch" (op. cit., p. 257) spoke of "Masters" who can respond or not, as they please, to the (mental)

"Call" of mortals, and added, "but the ordinary soul is very sensitive to the call of those it loved on earth". Later (op. cit., p. 285) he pointed out that "the power of creative imagination" is stronger in incarnate than in discarnate souls and gave the following reason: "A solid body is a resistive base, a powerful lever, from which the will can project the things conjured up by the imagination."

After "Scott", the "communicator" of Jane Sherwood (*The Psychic Bridge*, Rider & Co. Ltd., p. 31), used her hand to produce scripts, she began to question the wisdom of the proceedings. "Scott" said, "You forget that, in the beginning, it was *your* thought that could be so easily impressed on *my* brain." [This was, on the one hand, because her physical body, with its vehicle of vitality, acted after the fashion of a gun-emplacement from which *her* thoughts were projected and, on the other hand, the "brain" of "Scott's" Soul Body was no longer "insulated", "buffered", "screened", or "blinkered" by a physical body, and he received mental impressions very readily].

Nearly a century ago, the "communicator" of Mrs Cora L. V. Tappan (*Discourses*, J. Burns, 1875, p. 41) pointed out that, since communication involves "beings of a different order from yourselves—organized differently [i.e. with a Soul Body only], they must employ some instrumentality whereby they may reach your mind. Certain persons are endowed by nature with a physical organization which permits them to be used as mediums between the two worlds" [=their "semi-physical" vehicle of vitality is loosely associated with the physical body].

A famous American lady, Mrs Wright Sewall, who had "never read" psychic literature, produced a book entitled *Neither Dead nor Sleeping* (Watkins, 1921). On

p. 311 of this book her "communicator" described the process of communication. He began by describing the bodily constitution of mortals as follows: "It is the inhalation of the ether within the atmosphere by the mind within the body that keeps the mind in vital relation with its encasement [=the 'ether'=vehicle of vitality, is the necessary bridge or link between mind or Soul, which uses the Soul Body, and the physical body. Without the link that is represented by the *vehicle of vitality*, the Soul Body, and therefore the Soul, could not affect, or be affected by, the physical body]. Death is the severing of the etheric bond. ... The tenant thus dis-embodied finds itself to be still itself, moved by the same emotions, etc., as when incarnated. *It finds every emotion and spiritual aptitude quickened by its release from the flesh.* ... Ether ... is the medium of communication between the two spheres [earth and 'Paradise']. ... *Communication is made possible by the fact that ether [=vehicle of vitality] which is common to both the ante- and post-mortem planes [earth and 'Hades'] has the quality which enables it to receive and transmit vibrations of all kinds. ...*"

Estelle Stead published "communications" received from her father, W. T. Stead, recorded by the psychic Pardoe Woodman, in *The Blue Island*, Experiences of a New Arrival Beyond the Veil (Hutchinson & Co., 1922). Although she herself did not receive the "communications", her presence was a help. She stated: "Father always prefers me to be present, as if I am not he seems to have more difficulty, and very rarely will attempt writing. He explains the necessity of my presence in this way: he and I are so much *en rapport* that *he is able to draw much power from me. I act as a connecting-link* and form a sort of battery between him and Mr Woodman. I merely sit passive, while Mr Woodman writes."

Mrs C. A. Dawson-Scott (*From Four Who are Dead*, Arrowsmith, 1926, pp. 13–19) exemplified "co-operation" in order to achieve "communication". When in a passive condition, she saw in front of her "a dark tunnel" and, when she entered it, "stepped into a new world" where she met Mr Craven, the discarnate husband of a friend. Near him was Mrs Craven, out of her body (to which she was connected by "a twisted rope of white material", i.e. the "silver cord"), but Mrs Craven was so greatly depressed that she saw neither her husband nor Mrs Dawson-Scott. The next day, the latter again "entered the tunnel" [=left her physical body] and again saw Mr Craven in "the next world". He was trying to relieve his wife's depression. Mrs Dawson-Scott said, "It was as if he were saying, 'If only she could know I am here!'" [=that he had survived the death of his physical body and was near and trying to comfort her]. He urged Mrs Dawson-Scott, "Tell her!" She replied, "She would not believe me: I have no proof!" He repeated, "Tell her!" Mrs Dawson-Scott delayed telling Mrs Craven. By the time she did so, Mrs Craven had received the same message through another friend.

"Wilberforce" (*Letters from the Other Side*, Watkins, 1919, pp. 145–151) explained that, after he had been communicating for some time, he had to cease because *"the tenuous matter [=ectoplasm from the vehicle of vitality of the psychic], out of which the thread of communication is spun, becomes used up"*. If he continued in these circumstances, it "would mean using the psychic's life forces". He advised as follows: "As a general rule, avoid the exercise of such faculties where other means are available. Few are fitted to experiment in these directions, as *few possess abundant or super-abundant vitality.* You need your strength to cope with your daily activities. ...

Abstain from all attempts in this direction. Should your presence become ... really essential, you would be enabled to be visible or perceptible in the form adequate to accomplish the desired end. You need not yourself be aware of your beneficient ministrations. Few brains can accommodate the mundane and the ultra-mundane activities at one and the same time. Most so-called mediums have little preoccupation of the intellectual order, and so are free for the manifestation of the psychic faculties, rarely truly spiritual, though often mistaken for such."

SUMMARY—*Our physical body (with its vehicle of vitality) retards our thoughts and emotions but it thereby also strengthens them—it acts after the manner of a resistant base or gun-emplacement. The "semi-physical" vehicle of vitality is a necessary "link", or "bridge", between the living (who use a physical body) and the normal dead (who use the "super-physical" Soul Body).*

REASON—*Some people (who may be unaware of the fact) have a vehicle of vitality that is loosely associated with the physical body and they tend to be "mediumistic", able to receive "communications". (The faculty can, of course, be either deliberately developed or entirely neglected. This depends upon the person concerned. Development has certain advantages, but carries definite responsibilities.)*

CHAPTER V

"CO-OPERATION" AS DESCRIBED
BY PSYCHICAL RESEARCHERS, Etc.

WE have seen that supposed *discarnate communicators* say that we mortals (especially if somewhat psychic and especially during deep sleep) can, usually without being aware of the fact, give help to (1) other mortals, (2) the dying, (3) the newly-dead and (4) the "earthbound" —"spirits in prison". These particular statements necessarily came through mediums, sensitives or psychics, i.e. indirectly, and not directly, and we ask, "Did they, as claimed, come from the still-living 'dead' or were they sub-conscious products of the mediums, sensitives or psychics concerned?"

The very similar testimony of *the dying* concerning the help that they can give to the "earthbound" was not transmitted through mediums, sensitives or psychics. Nevertheless, the dying are not in a normal condition and what they may say should not be accorded much weight.

The identical testimony of *psychics* concerning the help that mortals (especially if somewhat psychic and during sleep) can give to (1) other mortals, (2) the dying, (3) the newly-dead and (4) the "earthbound", like those of the dying, are at least first-hand. The same applies to the testimonies of *astral projectors*.

We now turn to testimonies that clearly accord with those mentioned above; these cannot be dismissed as of sub-conscious origin. They consist of observations and deductions that were made by psychical researchers, etc.

1. "CO-OPERATION" THAT HELPS OTHER MORTALS

Dr Horatio Dresser, PH.D. (*The Open Vision*, George G. Harrap, p. 333), the American philosopher who was averse from mediumship and did not seek "communications" but "guidance", nevertheless was often aware of "co-operation" between discarnate helpers and mortals. He gave instances: "For example, he [the discarnate helper] might prompt mortal friends to bring me the books which I should read and these friends might bring me what I needed without being aware that they were participating in my work." He added, "*In fact, one of the profoundest reasons for believing in guidance is seen in the fact of minds co-operating incidentally to carry out a work without knowing they are making such contributions.* ... We are open in spirit both to friends in the flesh and to those beyond it. When engaged in a piece of work requiring guidance on *the future life*, we are more likely to receive it from *the spiritual world*. When facing *moral issues demanding self-mastery*, we are more likely to walk with *God alone*."

F. W. H. Myers (*Human Personality*, Longmans, Green & Co., 1907, p. 238) drew attention to several cases in which he suggested "co-operation". In the case of Mrs Green (*Proc.*, S.P.R., V, 420), two women were drowned under peculiar circumstances. A friend of theirs had a vision of the scene. The vision, however, did not (as is usual) occur at the time of the event but many hours later. *The vision occurred, in fact, at a time when another person, one who was deeply interested in the drowned ladies, heard of the tragedy.*

Myers suggested that the vision was "telepathed" by the "dead" ladies, but that the telepathic impression was too feeble to be recieved until it had been "*reinforced by some vivid current of emotion arising in living minds"*. As certain "communicators" suggested, the physical body, with its vehicle of vitality, acted as a "resistive base" or gun-emplacement, strengthening the originally weak impression.

It should he noted that there is no evidence that the one who was "deeply interested" in these ladies was aware, either at the actual time or later, that his "co-operation" had been used.

Myers (op. cit., 1907, p. 245) said, "Unless the actual evidence be disallowed in a wholesale manner, we should be forced, I think, to admit *the continued action of the departed* as a main element in these apparitions.

"I do not say as the only element. I myself hold, as already implied, that *the thought and emotion of living persons does largely intervene, as aiding or conditioning the independent action of the departed.* I even believe that it is possible that, say, an intense fixation of my own mind [= 'Call'] on a departed spirit may aid that spirit to manifest at a special moment—and not even to me, but to a percipient more sensitive than myself."

The "red scratch" case (*Proc.* S.P.R., VI, p. 17), also published by Myers (op. cit., 1907, p. 405), is best explained as an example of "co-operation". The sister of Mr F. G., of Boston, died. About a year later he became a commercial traveller and went on a trip to the West. He was booking orders at noon when he became aware that someone was sitting nearby. He turned and distinctly saw his "dead" sister. He sprang up and called her name, but the figure vanished. He said, "I was near enough to touch her. She appeared as if *alive*. Her eyes looked kindly and perfectly naturally into mine. Her skin was life-like."

"F.G." continued, "Now comes the most remarkable confirmation of my statement, which cannot be doubted by those who know what I state actually occurred ... I told them of a bright red line or *scratch* on the right-hand side of my sister's face, which I had distinctly seen. When I mentioned this, my mother rose trembling to her feet and nearly fainted away, and as soon as she sufficiently recovered her self-possession, with tears streaming down her face, she exclaimed that I had indeed seen my sister, as no living mortal but herself was aware of that scratch, which she had accidentally made while doing some little act of kindness after my sister's death.

"She said she well remembered how pained she was to think she should have, unintentionally, marred the features of her dead daughter, and that, unknown to all, how she had carefully obliterated all traces of the slight scratch with the aid of powder, etc., and that she had never mentioned it to a human being, from that day to this. In proof, neither my father nor any of our family had detected it, and positively were unaware of the accident—*yet I saw the scratch as bright as if just made.*

"So strangley impressed was my mother that, even after she had retired to rest, she got up and dressed, came to me and told me *she knew at least* that I had seen my sister.

"A few weeks later my mother died, happy in her belief that she would rejoin her daughter in a better world."

Commenting on this remarkable case, Zoë Richmond (*Evidence of Purpose*, G. Bell & Sons Ltd., 1938, p. 42) stressed the fact that had his mother (who knew of the red scratch) "seen" her daughter it would have been less evidential; the brother knew nothing of the accident. The suggestion is that the girl intentionally appeared to her brother rather than to her mother. But it seems more likely that the brother was more sensitive than the mother—he "co-operated" with his sister, preparing their mother for her "passing".

It may be added that Zoë Richmond (op. cit., 1938) in the Introduction to her book, said "even in this small collection" of cases, "there seems some evidence that *personal intentions [of mortals] can be used by some synthesizing power with intentions of its own, without the volition of the individual, as if something were saying to the percipient, 'How do you account for this—isn't it rather unusual? Please pay attention!'* " She continued, "And the fact that attention was paid by all these people in different ways, and that their experiences did arouse interest, and much more than this in some cases, shows that this wider intention was not fruitless."

On p. 53 of her book, Zoë Richmond gave the case of a doctor from *Journ.* S.P.R., XXVI, p. 117 and concluded, "The impression seems to convey an intention of lessening the distress of impending trouble [to mortals], if it could not avert the accident". She suggested that *"the doctor's willingness to serve people rendered him specially sensitive to the type of warning he gave"*. This agrees with the statements of "communicators".

Dorothy Grenside (*The Meaning of Dreams*, G. Bell & Sons Ltd., 1923, p. 117) cited three examples of "co-operation", while out of the body, by a woman-lecturer, *none of which the latter remembered*. One was as follows. The lecturer, having given an address in a London suburb, was afterwards approached by a woman, a complete stranger, who said that a few nights before, she had *"a kind of waking dream"*: in this, a woman who was then unknown to her had entered the room holding a Miss West, a friend of the narrator, by the hand. Miss West was greatly in need of comfort and support. The lady who had brought her was the lecturer. But *the lecturer remembered nothing* of the matter.

The two other examples were very similar to this: in each case this lecturer had "co-operated" to help a stranger, had been seen, out of the body, by another stranger, but she herself had not brought the experience through the brain into "normal" consciousness.

2. "CO-OPERATION" THAT HELPS THE NEWLY-DEAD

Some psychical researchers give the same reason why mortals are better able to influence the "newly-dead" than are Spirits in "Paradise" conditions. Dr Hereward Carrington (*Your Psychic Powers*, Kegan Paul, 1920, p. 57) said, "Many of the 'spirits' who have passed over, being nearer earth than 'Heaven' [here ='Paradise'], soon after their transition, are more easily reached by the living than by other spirits—so far as comfort, advice and assistance are concerned—and, for this reason, prayers of the living are often a great help to those who have recently 'passed over' and are extremely 'earthbound' by reason of their mental and moral characteristics."

Léon Denis (*Here and Hereafter*, Rider & Co. Ltd., 1910, p. 252) held that mortals can aid the newly-dead (whether relatively undeveloped or not). He stated, "Our evocations [='Call'] attract the attention of the deceased and facilitate their corporeal liberation. Our ardent prayers ... enlighten them."

3. "CO-OPERATION" THAT HELPS THE "EARTHBOUND"

The Revd. C. L. Tweedale (*Man's Survival After Death*, Grant Richards, 1909, p. 111) gave an instance in which a woman poisoned herself, died and found that she was "earthbound". She "communicated" two days later and asked for prayers on her behalf. Tweedale commented, "I have personally received similar requests for prayers on several occasions from the departed ... Similar requests for prayer have been received by many other investigators. There is abundant evidence to show that *the departed are in some instances helped and enabled to make their first advance in the spirit world not so much by angel ministry as by the sympathy, forgiveness and prayer of those still in this mortal life.*" [The latter, like the "earthbound", possess a vehicle of vitality].

Writing in *Light* (LXXXII, 1962, p. 40) Charlotte M. Waterlow, M.A., pointed out that "The rational mind, in showing modern man that he can be free from what is commonly called 'superstition', i.e. childish dependence on real or imaginary spirits, has cleared the way for a new relationship between mortals and spirits, an adult relationship, namely, 'soul communion'. The immature person, being ego-centred and self-isolated [separate from others not in fact but in his own thinking] tends to treat others, whether incarnate or discarnate, as outside himself, and thus he *communicates* rather than *communes* with them—there is not *vital contact* ... But in communion between mature souls there is that complete interchange of *life-force*, that complete blending of consciousness which is love, and which develops and enhances the personality of each ... *And as soul-communion between angel and mortal takes place (whether or not accompanied by external phenomena such as clairvoyance and clairaudience) the angels will be enabled thereby to enter into the murky psychic realm of the earthbound spirits* [='Hades'] *to release and heal them.*"

Dr Carl A. Wickland (*Thirty Years Among the Dead*) described many "rescues" of "earthbound" souls over a period of thirty-five years. One discarnate helper claimed that he co-operated in "missionary work" which consisted in "waking-up" spirits. Wickland observed: "It may be asked why *advanced* intelligences [in 'Paradise' conditions] do not take charge of 'earth-bound' spirits and convert them without having their first control, a psychic intermediary?" He answered: *"Many of these ignorant spirits cannot be reached by the intelligent spirits until they come in contact with physical conditions.* Then they are compelled to realize their own situation and are started on road to progression. Many controlling ['earthbound'] spirits act as if demented and are difficult to reason with, this condition being due to the *false doctrines, fixed ideas, etc.* Upon realizing their true condition [=that they have died], many [of the 'earthbound'] spirits experience a sensation of dying, which signifies that they are losing control [=quitting the body] of the psychic." [That is—they experience death by proxy! It is the *medium's* physical body, not their own, that they experience shedding].

Léon Denis (loc. cit.) arrived at the same conclusions in France as did the lawyer Randall and the medical man Carl Wickland in America, the zoologist Fitz-simons in South Africa, the banker Arthur Findlay in Great Britain, etc. He pointed out that people who do not realize the existence of discarnate souls do not offer aid to the needy "backward" ones (i.e. "earthbound" =in "Hades"). He gave the same reason as the others. *"The backward spirit, having more affinity to man than to those spirits that are pure* [=in 'Paradise'] *because of their fluidic constitution* [=the presence of the vehicle of vitality] *which is as yet coarse, are by that very fact rendered more amenable to our influence."*

4. "CO-OPERATION" THAT HELPS COMMUNICATION, ETC.

Professor William James suggested a theory of "co-operation" in endeavouring to explain the nature of "guides" (or "controls") in mediumship. After a study of the "Hodgson" "control" of Mrs Piper, James thought that the desire to communicate by the surviving Hodgson might co-operate with the desire to impersonate on the part of the trance-personality of Mrs Piper (the former providing true indications of survival and the latter any irrelevant "sub-conscious" materials added by the medium). James (*Proc.*, S.P.R., 43, p. 43) said, "*The two wills might thus strike up a sort of partnership and reinforce each other.*" (See also Rosalind Heywood, *The Sixth Sense*, Chatto & Windus, 1959, p. 67).

This idea seems to be related to the Persona Theory advanced and developed with great skill and considerable success by Professor Hornell Hart in an important work entitled *Enigma of Survival*, Rider & Co. Ltd., 1959, p. 189.

Dr R. C. Johnson, in his excellent book *Psychical Research*, English Universities Press Ltd., 1955, p. 136 (as in his *The Imprisoned Splendour*, Hodder & Stoughton, 1953, p. 284) adopted, with important modifications, the interesting ideas concerning the production of apparitions, whether of the living or of the dead, that were advanced by G. N. M. Tyrrell (*Apparitions*, 1953, the "Seventh Myers Memorial Lecture 1943" Duckworth & Co., 1953): these ideas involve "co-operation" between an "agent" and a "percipient". Johnson said, "There is always apparently an agent—the initiating mind. In cases of haunting this may also be true … The agent initiates it and supplies the original emotional energy to create and sustain it. The percipient, however, plays a part which may not be quite so passive as it appears to be on conscious levels. One of the notable things is that where the apparition is of the agent's person, the agent cannot be supposed to do more than create the general idea of himself in a certain place. None of us know in detail what we look like from a point in space external to our body. The percipient's mind clearly plays a part in this. Likewise the apparition often does things the agent had not envisaged, and shows a knowledge of the environment in which it appears, which the agent's conscious mind does not possess. It would seem as though there is *a collaboration* below the conscious level between certain functions of levels of the two minds, those of agent and percipient ... *The Tyrrell type [of apparition] is subjective and psychically created by co-operative activity between the agent's and percipient's mind ... The little dramatic scene is a joint construction of certain levels of the two minds."*

The Gordon Davis case (*Proc.* S.P.R., XXXV) may here be mentioned. In it a living man (presumably partially exteriorized in his "double", from his physical body) communicated by *direct voice* through Mrs Blanch Cooper. The medium's normal "control" twice interrupted the communications, complaining that Davis was too strong for the medium. At the end of the sitting the latter was exhausted, symptoms which she had not experienced with other "communicators". Hence, at the second sitting, the "control" would not allow Davis to communicate directly; she questioned him herself (the whispered conversation between her and Davis being audible) and transmitted the answers to the sitter. Professor E. Bozzano (*Discarnate Influence in Human Life*, Watkins, 1938) made this comment: "Now the interesting fact of the spirit of Gordon Davis having proved too strong for the medium would suggest that this happened owing to *the 'psychical invasion of an incarnate spirit, who carried with him psychic elements [=Soul Body] strongly impregnated with earthy fluids [=ectoplasm from the vehicle of vitality]'."* Bozzano, like many communicators, regarded the total physical body (which includes the vehicle of vitality with its ectoplasm, vitality or nervous force) as acting like a *gun-emplacement.*

Hewat McKenzie (*Quart. Trans. B.C.P.S.*, V, 1926, p. 58) regarded communication in the Gordon Davis case as illustrating what we call "co-operation": he learned that Dr Soal (the "sitter" who obtained the messages from Davis of whose death he had been erroneously told) "had often thought sympathetically, and even with a degree of affection, of the communicator, since the rumour of his death had reached him". McKenzie continued, "This thought was a very real thing, therefore, as far as Dr Soal was concerned, and doubtless, owing to his strong mediumistic powers, *he became the psychic link between himself and the living Gordon Davis,* although at the time he had no actual knowledge of him." He added, "Spirit intercourse seems largely influenced between the mortal and the spirit, and *creates the magnetic link* which draws them together ... " The present point is that McKenzie considered that *Dr Soal, the "sitter", "co-operated" with Blanch Cooper, the medium, to produce communications.* (The fact that they were erroneously regarded as emanating from a "dead" instead of a "living" man is beside the point. There are numerous instances of communication emanating from people who were in physical embodiment.)

The Revd. E. K. Elliott (*Journ.* S.P.R., 1895), at sea, on the night of January 14th, 1847, "dreamed" that he received a letter from his *uncle,* dated January 3rd ("Jan. 3 was very black, as if intended to catch my eye"). It said that his *brother* had died. The next morning Elliott recorded the "dream" in his diary. Returning to England, he found that his brother had, in fact, died on January 3rd. We interpret this case as follows. The newly-dead brother tried to communicate his change of condition of Mr Elliott, but either the "power" was insufficient, or Mr Elliott was too insensitive, or both. However, the discarnate brother was able to get the "co-operation" of the incarnate uncle (whose vehicle of vitality was relatively loose).

There is much evidence that the ectoplasmic emanations of mortals (especially those of people whose vehicle of vitality is somewhat loose) impregnate walls, furniture and other physical objects (hence, doubtless, the possibility of object-reading or psychometry). Thus, "co-operation" may occur indirectly, i.e. without drawing on the "co-operator" himself. An example is as follows: Capt. Campbell, in the barracks at Armagh, Ireland, had a "dream" in which Major Hubbersty, a fellow officer whom he had not seen for eighteen months and who was not a particular friend, fell forward as though dying. It turned out that the Major had died in Penzance on the date of the "dream". Campbell observed, "A very curious fact is that *the dream occurred to me in the very same room in the barracks that Major Hubbersty used to occupy*." (F. Podmore, *Apparitions and Thought-transference*, Walter Scott Ltd., London). Cornilier's *The Survival of the Soul* (Kegan, Paul, 1921) contains similar cases.

W. H. Harrison (*Light*, 1924) gave an example of "co-operation" that involved two sleepers. One of them, "A", awakened suddenly and saw an apparition; the other, "B", remained so deeply asleep that he could not, at first, be aroused. The suggestion is that the discarnate visitant who appeared induced a particularly deep sleep in "B" in order to withdraw ectoplasm from his vehicle of vitality.

Case No. 513 of *Phantasms of the Living*, by E. Gurney, F. W. H. Myers and F. Podmore (Kegan Paul, 2 vols., 1886) and the well-known case of Lord Tyrone's apparition to Lady Beresford also appear to involve "co-operation".

F. W. H. Myers (*Human Personality*, vol. II, p. 332) cited the case of Mrs "V". She was in India. Between 1.00 and 3.00 a.m. she awoke to see a vision of her sister who lived in London and, so far as she knew, was alive. She told her husband. A telegram arrived at 8.00 a.m. giving the news of her death. Mrs "V", whose husband was well known to Myers and who held an important post in India, had had other similar experiences (too private for publication).

Eleven years after the above-mentioned episode, Mrs "V" saw her dead sister again when she was present in Church at the confirmation of her sister's boy. The figure stretched her arms above the boy as though blessing him. Mrs "V" was evidently psychic, and her next experience suggests "co-operation". Mrs "V" was in India. The husband of an acquaintance was dangerously ill at an hotel some five miles away. She often went to enquire about him. One evening, when the doctor thought his condition was critical, she remained with the wife and then returned home at 10.00 p.m.

About midnight the venetian curtains in her room began to shake, knockings were heard, and she heard the name "A.B." (which name was unknown to her) whispered. Mrs "V" was persuaded not to go out. When Mrs "V" got to the hotel in the morning, she found that the man had died at 10 a.m. His wife told her (1) that she had wished to send for her during the night and (2) that *the name "A.B." was the name of her brother who had died seven years before.*

The suggestion is that the "dead" brother of her acquaintance had tried to "co-operate" with Mrs "V" (who was psychic) to aid his sister (who was not). She had, however, been dissuaded.

Dr James Hyslop (*Contact with the Other World*, 1919) pointed out: "If we believe in telepathy, we believe in a process which makes possible the invasion of a personality by someone at a distance." In much the same way, we point out that if we believe in the existence of the Soul Body and its occasional extrusion, or projection, from its physical counterpart, we believe in something which makes possible the invasion of a vacated physical body by another Soul Body. This would not be accepted by many modern psychologists, but Professor William James believed that this sort of theory "will have its innings again". The difficulty is, of course, to draw satisfactory distinctions (if such exist) between such cases (of "possession", or in extreme instances, "obsession") and the familiar cases of multiple personality.

Professor William McDougall, Professor of Psychology at Harvard, and Dr Nandor Fodor (op. cit., 1933, p. 280) were both inclined to regard the Miss Beauchamp case (in which all the personalities but one that were associated with one physical body were "squeezed" out of existence) as one of "possession" rather than multiple personality.

Dr Gustave Geley (*From the Unconscious to the Conscious*, Collins, 1920) also considered that mediumistic personalities differ from multiple personalities—"there is in mediumship an action of intelligent entities, distinct from the medium". More recently, the greatest of present-day philosophers, Professor C. J. Ducasse, Emeritus Professor of Philosophy at Brown University, U.S.A. (*A Critical Examination of the Belief in a Life After Death*, Thomas, Springfield, Ill., U.S.A., 1961, p. 17) has concluded that in most cases of apparent "possession" the "possessor" is merely a dissociated, normally repressed portion (a "split") of the total personality of the individual concerned—that this applies, e.g. to the cases of the Revd. Ansel Bourne, Miss Beauchamp and Doris Fischer. But, he maintained, *in "a few others", the "possessor" gives more or less clear and abundant evidence of being an individual who had died some time before"*, e.g. the Watseka Wonder (Mary Lurancy Vannum) concerned Mary Roff, who had died at the age of eighteen in the year 1865. (Lurancy Vennum was born in 1864 and "possession" began in 1877). In view of *other* evidence for survival, Professor Ducasse inclines to the conclusion that this did represent "possession" by the "dead", i.e. that this (and a few other similar cases) do constitute evidence for survival. It may be added that Professor Ducasse's *general* conclusion regarding survival is as follows: "The balance of the evidence so far obtained is on the side of the reality of survival ... ".

CONCLUSIONS

It is clear that many of the most eminent psychical researchers, etc., have evisaged the hypothesis of "co-operation" to account for phenomena identical in nature to those mentioned, entirely independently, by (a) astral projectors, (b) psychics, (c) the dying and (d) supposed communicators—helping mortals, the newly-dead, the "earthbound" and "communicators".

It is true that the "communicators" (those who have given most information about this possible activity) are in the weakest position, since their depositions come to us indirectly, through mediums. But the fact that these indirect statements are identical with the testimonies given directly by astral projectors, psychics, and the dying, added to the fact that they correspond to the hypotheses of numerous psychical researchers, has been overlooked. It is surely significant. The inescapable inference seems to be that *these* "communications", though received indirectly, were nevertheless genuine.

It is the practice of many would-be critics of psychic matters, who fondly suppose they are playing an unanswerable card, to ask "communicators": "Tell us something we don't know!" Well, this matter of "co-operation" is among matters declared by "communicators" years before psychical research began, that appears to be genuine and that the would-be critics failed to observe, much less appraise. (Other instances of this state of affairs were mentioned in *The Supreme Adventure*, pp. 8, 184).

The "co-operation" which we have exemplified above has been invariably for beneficent ends. Since both incarnate and discarnate souls include those whose intentions, so far from being beneficent, are maleficent, if the case for "co-operation" rested on descriptions of helpful activities only, it would be weak: but there are also in "communications" many warnings against hurtful "co-operation". We are warned that, while people whose feelings and intentions are definitely good tend (usually unconsciously) to "co-operate" for good, those whose emotions, desires and motives are selfish, sensual and evil tend (also usually unconsciously) to "co-operate" for evil purposes. Hence it is a "law", as St Paul (Rom. viii, 28) pointed out, that "All things work together for good to them that love God", and by the same "law" all things work together for evil for those who are definitely evil—only so, through the harm and suffering that malevolence brings, can the wicked be induced eventually to alter their ways.

Many "communicators" insist that incarnate souls and discarnate souls (the "living" and the "dead") affect each other, so that they can either encourage and expedite or discourage and retard each other's moral and spiritual development. Such statements are often made in general terms and sometimes refer particularly to the execution of criminals. We cite examples.

"Philip", the discarnate son of Dr Alice Gilbert (*Philip in the Spheres*, Aquarian Press, 1952, p. 101), said that when the evil men who were responsible for the atrocities of the concentration camps were hanged *"they could be used to foment evil, being so fresh from earth"*. [i.e. retaining the vehicle of vitality]. He explained it thus: "When you expel such fiends from earth, you are expanding their power for harm. In the flesh their radiating power is, to an extent, insulated and confined."

The "communicator" of H. A. and F. H. Curtiss (*Realms of the Living Dead*, 1917, p. 111) said, "The execution of a criminal merely removes his hampering physical body, which at least limited his evil activities to the physical world. Destroying his physical body sets him free in the astral world [here = 'Hades'], embittered, able to throw his force over any mind which is *open* to such thoughts. He seeks to wreak his vengeance and gratify his desires by controlling and obsessing as many *sensitive persons* as possible—those with auras sufficiently open to permit his entrance into their consciousness."

Many other "communicators" take this attitude towards capital punishment. They say that, though the criminal who is executed passes from mortal sight, he is still "near earth" (in a composite body, one that consists of *the "semi-physical" vehicle of vitality* as well as the "super-physical" Soul Body) and consequently "near" to mortals, so that he may affect potential psychics. If he is actuated by a sense of grievance, desire for revenge, sensuality, etc., he may "tempt"— *and may himself be tempted by* mortals in whom similar tendencies are dominant, those who brood over such matters (Phil. iv, 8). This would involve "co-operation" for evil purposes, even though it took place involuntarily and unconsciously. If men of goodwill sometimes "entertain", and "co-operate" with, "angels" unawares (Heb. xiii, 2), men of evil-will must "entertain", and "co-operate" with, "devils" (in the sense of wicked discarnate souls) also unawares. We note that F. W. H. Myers (*Human Personality*) found "nothing worse than living men ... "

Habitual and predominant emotions, desires and thoughts form the basis of telepathic contact not only between mortals but also between incarnate and discarnate souls and there is an effect comparable to "boosting" in electrical phenomena.

These processes take place automatically and we are seldom directly aware of them. But the line of separation between the "sub-conscious" and the "conscious" is neither sharp nor constant and it is especially shifting in people who tend to be psychic. "Communicators" declare that an unconscious attraction can grow into an association which is conscious on one or both sides. On this new suggestion, whether "alive" or "dead", people are not separated from each other, as we tend to imagine. It would be more true (we are told by "communicators") to say with St Paul (Ephes. iv, 25) that we are "members one of another", so that no one can escape being his "brother's keeper" (Gen. iv, 9). In this context the rationale of the Master's injunctions (Matt. v, 44, Mark xii, 31, Matt. vii, 12) becomes clear.

"Mr Thomas", communicating to his son the Revd. C. Drayton Thomas, (*The Life Beyond Death with Evidence*, Collins, 1928), said, "While unprogressed ones might *suggest* evil to men's minds, they have no power to *force* men in any way. Unwholesome [mortal] companions are more to be feared than any who have left the earthly body: the latter can use mental influence only; those on earth can also use money, alluring surroundings, etc. *Tempters in the body are ten times more dangerous than invisible tempters.*"

G. G. André (*Morning Talks with Spirit Friends*, Watkins, 1926), another Englishman, was told, "No line of separation can be drawn between your world and ours. Everyone whilst in the body is in constant association with denizens of the spirit world, though he may not be conscious of their presence. It is well to be made aware of these subtle influences, so that they may be brought under the domination of your will."

"Hatch", a discarnate American lawyer, told Elsa Barker, *Letters of a Living Dead Man*, Rider & Co. Ltd., 1914) that it is especially when incarnate souls experience the intense emotion of love, hate or anger that they strongly attract these discarnate souls in whom the corresponding emotion is habitual. Thus: "When man is excited, exalted, or in any way intensified in his emotional life, the spirits draw near to him ... Hateful spirits stir up strife both here and on earth: they enjoy the excitement of anger in others. A man who has the habit of anger, even of fault-finding, is certain to be surrounded by evil spirits. Sometimes the impersonal interest in mere strife becomes personal: an angry spirit may find that, by attaching himself to a certain man, he is sure to get every day a thrill, or thrills, of angry excitement. Carried to its ultimate, it may become obsession ... The same law applies to lust, avarice, etc. *The power of the creative imagination is stronger in men wearing their earthly bodies than in spirits. A solid body is a resistant base, a powerful lever, from which the will can project those things conjured up by the imagination.*"

Cora L. V. Tappan (*Discourses*, J. Burns, 1875), another American, was told, "Mediums are sensitive, possessing external organizations that cannot resist, especially if not aware of it, an untoward influence ... against depression ... that often draws undeveloped spirits."

Although many "communicators" speak of the possibility, in very rare and extreme cases, of actual obsession, medical psychologists find few, if indeed any, cases that cannot be explained on the basis of well-known psychological principles. Be this as it may. Although actual obsession may be non-existent, pseudo-obsession, i.e. the community of thought and feeling of an incarnate soul with an undesirable, discarnate soul is undoubtedly a possibility.

People who tend to be dreamy also tend to be negatively psychic and should cultivate positive, out-going and social activities and not, either deliberately or unconsciously, increase their dreamy tendency. Prolonged debilitating illness, sudden and extremely severe shock, the abuse of drugs (including alcohol), may tend to turn non-psychics into (unconscious) psychics. Unless a person is of sound mind, has well-controlled emotions and is quite definitely actuated by the highest motives, he should not invite dissociation by the use of planchette, ouija board, "automatic writing", etc. To become psychic is to increase responsibilities and those who are unprepared must pay dearly for their temerity. To invite "co-operation" of this type is a grave step, not to be lightly taken.

The matter of community thought and feeling of the "living" and the "dead" just discussed, may seem disquieting to one who has not thought about such things. The question is not whether it is disquieting or not, but whether it is true or not. If it is true, forewarned is fore-armed. Knowledge is a safeguard; ignorance is false security: "Security is mortals' chiefest enemy", says Shakespeare. Moreover, it must be remembered that the "living" attract and influence the "dead" as much as—even more than—the "dead" attract and influence the "living". The "living" have the greater power in this respect. The physical body, with its semi-physical vehicle of vitality, give them both a negative and a positive advantage. The negative advantage is due to its relative sluggishness, its "slow vibrations", a factor which tends to protect, "shield", "screen" and "insulate" every "living" man from impressions coming from others, whether "alive" or "dead". The body is also a positive advantage, a source of strength, since the same quality causes it to operate after the manner of a gun-emplacement: thoughts, feelings and purposes sent out by the physically-embodied are far stronger and steadier than those sent out by discarnates: "action and reaction are equal and opposite".

Whether (and how far) we "co-operate": this depends largely on our total bodily constitution—on (a) how "loosely" the vehicle of vitality is associated with the dense physical body and (b) the degree to which the Soul Body is organized. Of these two factors, the former has no relationship whatever to the spiritual development, but the latter is so related. A spiritually-minded person tends to be, on account of the other factor, psychic (though we cannot reverse the proposition and say that a psychic person is necessarily a spiritually-minded person). *With whom we "co-operate"*: This is determined by our habitual thoughts and feelings. Temptation comes to all and is not in itself evil, but it must be ignored, replaced, or withstood. Definite, oft-repeated thoughts and images that are suffused with emotion have "co-operative" possibilities.

A number of Scriptural texts are clearly in line with these considerations. Jesus (Matt. v, 44) urged His followers: "Love your enemies and pray for your persecutors." St James (v. 13) said, "Is anyone among you in trouble? He should turn to prayer" and (v. 16) "Pray for one another and then you will be healed. A good man's prayer is powerful and effective."

In I Peter iii, 19, we are told that the newly-dead Jesus "went and made his proclamation to the imprisoned spirits".

The three chief disciples of the Master, named Peter, James and John—those whom He selected to be present at the raising of Jairus' daughter (Mark v, 37), at the Transfiguration (Mark ix, 2) and at Gethsemane (Mark xiv, 33) were *spiritually advanced* but they were probably also, on account of their bodily constitution (i.e. a "loose" vehicle of vitality), *naturally psychic* and therefore able to link "ministrant angels" with human beings, i.e. *to "co-operate"*. (This was also probably true, in Old Testament times: Abraham, Jacob and Moses were doubtless psychically (as well as spiritually) developed. They would therefore "co-operate" in preparing the way for the advent of the Master).

St Paul (Heb. xiii, 2) gave the following advice: "Show hospitality" and he added an inducement—"Some, by so doing, have entertained angels *without knowing it.*"

The Church of England, in the Prayer Book (in the Collect for St Michael and All Angels), states that, by God's appointment, angels (=messengers) "may succour and defend us on earth through Jesus Christ our Lord".

The importance of injunctions given by the Master, St James, St Paul, etc., as to the value of prayer has been realized by many.

The Curé d'Ars (1786–1859), who engaged in exceptionally prolonged and fervent prayer, observed to a friend, relative to the raising of money for charitable purposes, "One can get anything one wants if one fasts and watches long enough" [cf. Matt. xvii, 21—"This kind goeth not out but by prayer and fasting"]. As a result of his intercessions, the Curé built three chapels, established a home for poor children and another for friendless women. Whenever anything was needed—food, fuel, etc.—he prayed for it and it was provided.

George Müller (*The Life of Trust*) made an observation regarding prayer identical with that made by the Curé d'Ars. He established and maintained homes for boys in Bristol by prayer alone, never asking anyone (or allowing anyone to be asked) for anything. Those who sent contributions said that they suddenly felt an uncontrollable impulse to send Müller *a definite sum on a particular date*. It was exactly what had been requested in prayer.

The Revd. Christopher Blumhardt of Wurttemberg (1805–80) was the German equivalent of Müller in England and the Curé d'Ars in France. As with Müller, contributors felt impulses to send gifts.

Cases in which specific requests, made in prayer, are exactly answered, appear to represent examples of "co-operation". Those who are signally successful in this respect are doubtless more or less psychic.

A delightful little book, entitled *Gayneck, The Story of a Pigeon*, Puffin Story Book, 1944, described as most suitable for children of 9–14, concerns the life of a pigeon in the Himalayas. It includes incidental references to Buddhist teachings that correspond to some of those mentioned above. The Chief Lama not only showed the owner of the pigeon that he had supernormal knowledge of the latter's approaching visit to his monastery, but indicated how the knowledge was obtained. He said, "*It has been our practice for centuries to pray for all who sleep.*" This practice, he said, brought "the power to read some people's thoughts".

Dr J. W. Graham (*Journ. Friends' Historical Society*, 1933), the Quaker, similarly noted that prayer for and interest in the welfare of others tended to bring telepathic, clairvoyant and other super-normal experiences (through which the Quaker-fathers were able to help people in need). This seems to be a kind of safety-mechanism. Bodily constitution apart, whose who earnestly desire the welfare of others tend to have their ability to serve extended in this way: those, on the other hand, who are self-centred seldom believe in or try to develop such faculties—this is well, since they would inevitably injure both themselves and others:

"Their last state would be worse than the first" (Matt. xii, 45).

It is highly probable that most who read this book have engaged in "co-operation", though they are unaware of the fact, i.e, it has not entered everyday awareness, not been "remembered". There are many indications that this is the case (see Appendix II).

Our primary duty is not to enjoy super-normal experiences but to do the will of God and to be "faithful in that which is least" (Luke xvi, 10). Nevertheless, if we can "remember" a few instances in which we have ourselves "co-operated", our faith will be increased and with it our ability to "co-operate" further and more effectively.

THE ATTITUDE OF THE CHURCH

DR W. R. MATTHEWS, the Dean of St Paul's, pointed out in *The Daily Telegraph* that "Orthodox people make the mistake of supposing that they have all the truth and that nothing more can be known". Dr Cyril Alington similarly said: "To believe that any past generation held the monopoly of truth, or was able to give it final expression, is not only inconsistent with the teaching of history, but is a flat denial of the Holy Spirit, which has promised to guide us progressively into all truth." When Archbishop of Canterbury, Lord Fisher of Lambeth stated: "Set Church dogmas are nothing more than the experience of people who have preceded us, and all experience should be constantly under review. That is what the Church means when it says it is looking for the guidance of the Holy Spirit. The people who do harm to our Church are those who teach the dogma of a thousand years ago without any experience." (*Daily Mail*, November 30th, 1959). Turning to a Wesleyan divine, and to the positive rather than the negative of these matters, Dr Leslie Weatherhead considered that, "A careful, honest enquiry into psychic phenomena will yield even richer treasures for the well-being of man than physics, chemistry and biology have given us, vast though those treasures are" (*The Resurrection of Christ*).

Although the present writer has not had the advantage of theological training, he ventures to suggest that several matters could, with advantage, be considered by the Church. The first concerns the nature of man, a conception that necessarily affects not only the earth-life, but also the after-life. The "orthodox" view is that man consists of (physical) body, Soul and Spirit; hence when he dies he is bodiless for a time and he later acquires the Spiritual Body. This conception is not based on any *evidence* whatsoever, but upon certain Biblical texts. The conception which we advance, on the other hand, is based on actual *evidence* (which is cited in two books by the present writer, namely, *The Supreme Adventure*, James Clarke & Co. Ltd., 1961, and *The Study and Practice of Astral Projection*, Aquarian Press, 1961), and, in addition, it is also in accord with certain Spiritual texts (I Cor. xv, 35, 44). It is that our total bodily constitution includes *a hierarchy of three main bodies*, of which the physical body is the densest and least responsive to thought, feeling, etc. Just as a particular genus of animals, or of plants, may be considered by some scientists as comprising (say) three species, and by others as comprising (say) five or six species, so our total bodily make-up has been differently sub-divided by different people. It is most convenient to envisage three bodies, (1) the physical body (vivified by the vehicle of vitality"); (2) the Psychical or Soul Body, and (3) the Spiritual, Celestial or Divine Body.

Corresponding to these three bodies is *a hierarchy of three main "worlds", "realms", "spheres", "environments" or "conditions"*: it is considered from analogy with the physical body (which is "borrowed" from and eventually returned to, the physical world—Gen. iii, 19) that the Soul Body is "borrowed" from (and will eventually be returned to) the "Paradise" (="Garden of Eden") environment, which is part of the total earth, and that the Spiritual Body is "borrowed" from (and will eventually be returned to) the true "Heavens" of the Scriptures.

The fact that consciousness works through three (main) bodies, makes us appear to consist of *a hierarchy of three main selves*, each with its characteristic *"level" of consciousness*, i.e. the lesser, outer, lower, temporary everyday self or personality (with the normal "level" of consciousness, including instincts, emotions, reason, etc.), (2) the intermediate or psychic self, or soul (with a super-normal "level" of consciousness, including telepathic, clairvoyant and pre-cognitive abilities), and (3) the Greater, Inner, Higher, Eternal Self, or Over-Soul, of Emerson, etc., the Christ-in-You of St Paul (Col. i, 27), with a Spiritual, Cosmic or Mystical "level" of consciousness.

On this view, every man *already possesses* the bodily vehicles in which he will survive the death of his physical body, namely, a Soul Body and a (still more tenuous and reactive) Spiritual Body: he is not, as the "orthodox" suppose, bodiless for a time after death.— Just as, if our physical bodies are to be efficient instruments, they need food and exercise, so, if our Soul Bodies and Spiritual Bodies are to serve their respective functions, they require something that corresponds to physical food and exercise. They will then enable us to contact after-death conditions in which we can be useful to others and consequently happy.

The *"food"* of the Soul Body is clearly represented by our thoughts, emotions and willings. Every time we experience (and especially if we brood over and repeat) an emotion, such as love, fear, or anger, we have taken "food" into the Soul and affected, for good or ill, the Soul Body.

Every thought that is factually based, carefully considered, clearly formulated, carefully correlated with other, connected thoughts, and acted upon in daily life, is also "food" for the Soul Body. **Every** determined willing, allowing no exceptions ("Just this time!") also represents Soul-"food". A man whose emotions are strong and sincere, whose thoughts are well-defined, whose willings are inexorable and whose mental images are clear, i.e. one who has "fed" his Soul Body, will have an instrument that is of great value to him in this world and the next: he will be a helper. A man who has neglected to "feed" his Soul Body will experience weakness and frustration in this world and the next: he will be a hindrance.

Useful "co-operation" (described in the foregoing pages), corresponding to the *"exercise"* of the physical body, will be possible to those who have "fed" their Soul Bodies and, as the Master (Matt. xx, 12) said, "The man who has will be given more." This, in part, is because with thoughts and emotions like draws like.

Another form of "exercise" for the Soul Body consists in occasionally relaxing all physical tensions and then withdrawing the attention from physical sounds and sights and adopting a receptive attitude, i.e. using the "ears" and "eyes" of the Soul Body instead of those of the physical body.

The "food" of the Spiritual Body consists in self-less love, and the sincere search for moral and spiritual truth and beauty. Its "exercise" consists in expressing these things in words and deeds. These involve Eternal Life, whereas the activities of the Soul Body are con-fined to the immediate "next world" (="Paradise").

The Eternal, Greater Self, with its Spiritual Body, is a "branch" of the Cosmic Christ (John xv) who mediates the Love and Life which is the "Father". Hence all life and power comes from God, passes through the Spiritual Body, thence through the Soul Body and finally into the physical body. A mystical, dynamic or vital conception is mentioned many times in the Scriptures (John i, 6–14; iv, 15; v, 24–26; vi, 35–51; viii, 12; x, 10; xi, 25; xiv, 6; xv, 1–8; xvi, 21; Acts xvii, 1; John ii, 24–25; Rev. iii, 20). True health is from *"within"*. Jesus (Matt. v, 22) taught that our feelings and thoughts are primary and our actions secondary: hence that anger and abuse are evil and carry unpleasant consequences even when they do not issue in words and actions. Every psycho-analyst will agree with Solomon (Prov. iv, 23) that "Out of *the heart* are the issues of life".

The physical body, among other things, facilitates the formation of *habits* of thinking and feeling and willing and these habits continue (a) into the sleep-life, facilitating or retarding "co-operation" and (b) into the immediate after-life, affecting one's happiness (see *The Supreme Adventure*, p. 234). Just as our physical health depends upon innumerable (apparently) small and unimportant matters (connected with proper food, exercise, rest, change, etc.), so our moral and spiritual health depends on numerous (apparently) small and unimportant thoughts, feelings, etc. The Master (Matt. xii, 36) said, "I tell you this—there is not a thoughtless word that comes to men's lips but they will have to account for it ... "

Secondly, the Church teaches that there is no after-death state that is intermediate between the true "Heaven" of the Scriptures (the indescribable and supremely blissful Eternal Life with Christ and the Father) and "Hell" (the place of torment in which sinners will spend the after-life), i.e. that there is no preliminary condition that corresponds to the "Purgatory" of the Roman Church. The present writer (in *The Supreme Adventure*) has adduced *evidence* that there are a number of "worlds", "realms", "spheres", "environments" or "conditions", i.e. "many mansions", ranging from "Hell" (the place of torment) through "Hades" (a semi-dream world) to "Paradise" (an earth-like realm), all between the physical earth and the true Heavens that may be eventually attained. It is in this connection that our conception of hierarchies of three (main) bodies (each from a corresponding "world") and three (main) "selves" (each with its characteristic "level" of consciousness) is so helpful.

Omitting, for the sake of simplification, a consideration of the vehicle of vitality (and the "Hades" condition that corresponds to it), when a man sheds his physical body, i.e. dies, he has two bodies (the condition of which depends on his activities during physical embodiment): just as the physical body formerly "geared" the Greater Self down to the physical world, now the Soul Body "gears" it down to the "Paradise" environment. After some time in the latter, the Soul Body is shed, i.e. he "dies" to the "Paradise" world and he is then in the Spiritual Body and enters the true "Heavens". How satisfactorily he can react with this environment depends on how far he formerly exercised love and sought truth and beauty for their own sakes.

Thirdly, clergymen commonly suppose that "the silver cord" which was mentioned by Ecclesiastes (xii, 6) is merely a poetic fancy. The present writer has shown that there is *evidence* that it is an objective feature of great importance, a temporary extension of the Soul Body that permits "visits" to "the next world" (see *The Supreme Adventure*, pp. 120, 130, 188, also *Events on the Threshold of the After-Life*). It is important throughout earth-life and again in the process of transition.

Fourthly, our studies show that the (largely implicit) teaching that our loved ones who have died have "gone away", are "lost", "gone before", "asleep in Jesus", "at rest", etc., is actually false, and the (largely explicit) teaching that their present home is "far, far away" is the opposite of the truth. These are no mere academic matters; they are important to both the "living" and the "dead". If our loved ones are "asleep", "at rest" and "far, far away", they are neither in a condition—nor a position—to serve us and, by that same token, are beyond our help. The truth, we submit, is quite otherwise and, such being the case, both they and we have opportunities for spiritual advancement by mutual loving service—by "co-operation" in fact.

This was said not only by "communicators", psychics and astral projectors, but by clergymen and psychical researchers. Archdeacon Sharp (*The Spirit Saith*, p. 160) declared, "In my experience there is ample evidence to prove that the faithful departed for whom the Church bids us pray only that they may 'rest in peace', are, in fact, very busy people, guiding, inspiring, guarding and consoling by whatever means they are able. Amongst those whose activities are evident today are, to my knowledge, Archbishops, Bishops and saintly priests." He commented, "They might have more rest, and certainly more peace, if our leaders and Christians in general would listen to their witness to the truth instead of running away from them, and thus thwarting their efforts to fulfil their trust. Our perversity disturbs that peace that we pray to God to give them."

Again, Dr Sherwood Eddy (*You Will Survive Death*, Rinehart, 1950) observed that Dr Alfred Russell Wallace, the co-discoverer with Darwin, of evolution, who was originally a sceptic and materialist, but who found truth via psychical research, "believed he found not only God, but *a whole hierarchy of beings with infinite grades of power, of knowledge, of widsom, and everywhere the influence of higher beings upon lower. He found 'the universe requires the continuous co-ordinated agency of myriads of intelligences ... '* He did not think that such cases (i.e. of answered prayer as in the case of George Müller's faith orphanage) could be accounted for by chance. Wallace thought he could best account for them not by a solitary God who sat, as it were, at the great exchange of the universe, but *by the law of telepathy and the co-operation of spiritual beings in a vast unseen Kingdom of God"*.

Archbishop William Temple (*Nature, Man and God*, Macmillan, p. 457), like many others, confused the mere *survival* of bodily death (into realms that have time in some, though not in the strictly physical sense) with *Immortality or Eternal Life* (which is outside time in any sense). He could have emphasized the relative unimportance of the former without insisting that interest in it is of no value and even a spiritual danger. This attitude must have limited possible service by spiritually-minded people.

Temple said, "The great aim of all true religion is to transfer the centre of interest of concern from self to God." This is, of course, agreed. He continued, "The centre of all true religious interest is God, and self comes into it not as a primary concern which God must serve, but as that one thing which each can offer for the glory of God."

On this basis, Temple considered it "positively undesirable" that "*survival*" should be experimentally demonstrated because "This would bring the hope of *immortality* into the area of purely intellectual apprehension ... It would certainly, I think, make very much harder the essential business of faith, which is the transference of the centre of interest and concern from self to God." By this attitude he showed that he failed fully to realize God's plan of salvation which clearly involves *psychic* (as well as physical and other) *action* by those who *have* thus turned from interest in and concern about themselves to the worship of God to help others who have either not begun or are falteringly beginning to do the same.

The Revd. C. H. Dodd, the Director of the translation of the New English Bible (1961), in his Ingersoll Lecture on "The Communion of Saints" (p. 145), took up the position that, in a sense, is intermediate between Archbishop Temple's and that here maintained. He pointed out, "While Christianity attaches a high importance to the individual, it does so only within the framework of a conception of the imperishable society, which alone gives meaning to the life of the individual, whether in time or in eternity. *For Christianity the true seat of Eternal Life is the communion of saints, and the individual is held to be immortal within that communion ... Life in any important sense of the word, is shared life.*"

The coin has two sides; a man's interest and concern in himself can be transcended by service to other men and that is the proper outcome of the worship of God. Our point is that neither Archbishop Temple nor Dr Dodd appear to have considered that the dead are not "lost", or "gone before", and that we mortals can serve them (as well as other mortals) by psychic means, i.e. by "co-operation" during "out-of-the-body" experiences.

Bishop Paget (*Sermons on Saints' Days*, p. 305) said, "Angels are really no more to us than the fairies of heathen mythology ... Nevertheless, there stands the service of the Feast of St Michael and All Angels a witness against us. The doctrine is that those pure and blessed spirits, the Holy Angels, take an interest in us, that they 'succour and defend us'."

Cardinal John Henry Newman observed, "There

have been ages in which men thought too much of angels and honoured them so perversely as to forget the supreme worship due to God: that was the sin of 'a dark age'. But the sin of what is called 'an educated age', such as our own, is just the reverse—to account slightly of them, or not at all; to ascribe all we see around us not to their agency but to certain assumed laws of nature. *This is likely to be our sin in proportion as we are initiated into the learning of the world.*"

THE "REMEMBRANCE" OF "CO-OPERATIVE" ACTIVITIES

READERS of this book may, not unnaturally, ask, "If, as you say, I have left my physical body (in the Soul Body) during deep sleep and have 'co-operated' with 'ministering angels' on behalf of other souls, whether incarnate or discarnate, why am I unaware of the fact? Why do I fail to 'remember' out-of-the-body experiences whether they include 'co-operation' or not?" The answer is that these are *Soul-Body* activities and, in order to "remember" them (during earth-life) they must somehow pass through the brain of the *physical* body. If I pick up a poker and stir the fire, I feel its weight and its coldness; these sensations pass through the physical brain and they can, therefore, be readily recalled. But if (supposing the possibility) I perform an act with the Soul Body—this made no impression, or "trace", on the physical brain and it is most unlikely to be "remembered" through it when I re-enter the physical body (="wake up"). We cite a few statements on this matter.

I. STATEMENTS BY THE PSEUDO-DEAD

When Mrs K. M. Garrett almost died (so that her Soul Body was outside her physical body) she thought, "My face is whiter than the pillow!" She saw the nurse and the doctor approach her vacated physical body and inject something. But Mrs Garrett failed to "remember" this until twenty years later! (*Prediction*, August 1961, p. 17).

2. STATEMENTS BY ASTRAL PROJECTORS

Mrs Rhys Davids, D.LITT., M.A. (*What is Your Will?* Rider & Co. Ltd., pp. 67, 218) stated that she learned much while her Soul Body was "projected" from her physical body in deep sleep. But she could "remember" what she had learned only when she "*asked*" herself. She considered that her two "selves", (i.e. (1) the lesser, everyday self, or personality who uses the physical body and usually fails to "remember" out-of-the-body experiences, and (2) the psychic self or Soul who uses the Soul Body) are not, as might be thought, separate and distinct; on the contrary, *there is "one Self [the Greater or Eternal Self] playing on two instruments"*.

Mrs Davids, like many others, distinguished between mere dreams, fantasies that occur during periods of shallow sleep (and therefore chiefly as we enter or emerge from sleep) and genuine experiences in the released Soul Body that occur when the body is deeply unconscious. The present writer suggests that fantasies occur when consciousness is blurred by the vehicle of vitality (so that people who tend to be mediumistic, i.e. to have a "loose" vehicle of vitality, corresponding, it should be noted, to "Hades" conditions, are more given to dreaming just before or just after deep sleep).

Mrs Davids mentioned the man whose case was described by Dr Jung: this man "dreamed" that he saw "a sheet of calm water" [="Hades" conditions] which "became ruffled" and then his Soul Body experiences [corresponding to "Paradise" conditions] began. The man doubtless had a "loose" vehicle of vitality. The latter, with its fantasies, tends to blur any remembrance of Soul Body experiences.

Mrs Davids (like "communicators") held that mental

habits that we form through using the physical body
affect the Soul Body and therefore continue during our
sleep-life (and in the early after-life), producing genuine
out-of-the-body experiences as distinct from mere
dreams. She insisted that the chief things are to live an
outgoing (not a self-centred) life to "will with faith",
though without strain or effort. Occasions should be
made in which consciousness is abstracted from physical
sights and sounds and is focused inwards. This was
described as "The listening inner-looking will, a
waiting to receive while desiring only the truly worthy."
She advised that, while no particular word, image, etc.,
should be expected, there should be a general state of
bidding welcome: "Speak, brother, sister, I listen!"
and ever at the back of that, "Speak, Lord, thy servant
heareth!" Anything received should be written down at
once. Such exercises should not, of course, be under-
taken to excess or when fatigued. Mrs Davids was
convinced that (as might be expected) people who are
interested in the subject of the after-life tend to organize
the Soul Body and therefore to have out-of-the-body
experiences during deep sleep.

The "remembrance" of such experiences can be
developed up to a point—it is a matter of becoming
aware of, and of deliberately using, the Soul Body.
She herself claimed that, by this means, she had not
only "won a spiritual betterment" but also improved
her health, both physical and mental, and she urged
people to cultivate their own Soul Bodies, and thus
to make first-hand contact with "Angels" instead of
consulting mediums (to obtain information at second-
hand). Mrs Davids held that *genuine servers of mankind
and seekers after truth "are much oftener approached than is
realized by their fellows but few realize how much they lose
in being as barred doors to the aid that might be theirs"*.

3. STATEMENTS BY PSYCHICS

An American, Dr A. J. Davis (*The Principles of Nature*, 1847), held that discarnate souls and incarnate souls often commune together but that the latter are often unaware of, i.e. cannot "remember", such activities.

An English psychic, Robert James Lees (*The Gates of Heaven*, 1949, p. 155), said the same and added that "only the memory is at fault".

The great Swedish clairvoyant, Swedenborg (*Heaven and Hell from Things Seen and Heard*, 1758, p. 448), claimed that his Soul Body was carefully released from his physical body in such a way that he "might know *and remember*" his out-of-the-body experiences.

4. STATEMENTS BY "COMMUNICATORS"

A discarnate American general described what happens during the sleep of mortals to Anne Mannering Robins (*Both Sides of the Veil*, Sherman, French & Co., 1909, p. 153). He said, "Your spirit [here=Soul Body] goes out upon an ethereal cord [=the 'silver cord'– extension], just the same as the spirit [=Soul Body] of the 'Light' [=medium, in this case Mrs Piper] here departs [leaving the physical body unconscious] ... In sleep I talk with your spirit [in the Soul Body] just the same as I am talking with you now. Sometimes I almost feel you will *remember* it, but when your spirit becomes ... fully possessed of your body and mind, then it forgets."

Many English equivalents of these statements could be cited. The "communicator" of W. S. Montgomery Smith (*Two Worlds are Ours*, Rider & Co. Ltd., p. 143) said, "You have been with me in our home ... I bring you back ... One moment you are there and I am saying something to you and the next moment *you are awake and have forgotten.*" Again, "The earth would seem a miserable place after 'the other side'—awfully grey—if they were able to [remember], people couldn't be contented; half their minds would want the other place."

Kate Wingfield (*More Guidance from Beyond*, Philip Allen, 1925, p. 12) was told: "Heaven is as truly the home of the Soul as earth is the home of the body." Like many others, he insisted that earth-life is a training time for the Soul and "it should dimly remember its former estate, that the memory may act as a beacon to lead it back".

"Vettellini", the French "communicator" of P. E. Cornillier (*The Survival of the Soul*, Kegan Paul, Trench, Trubner & Co. Ltd., 1921), said the same—that, although we only dimly and occasionally "remember" our out-of-the-body experiences during deep sleep, they nevertheless emerge in everyday life as *intuitions* and intimations of immortality.

The "communicator" of *Letters from the Other Side* (Watkins, 1919, p. 14) gave a reason why we fail to remember our sleep-life. He told his mortal friend: "We meet during sleep ... But the physical brain is somewhat fragile and ... must not be taxed to record experiences that can wait for recognition" [i.e. wait until we are permanently disembodied].

G. Trevor (*Death's Door Opens*, 1950, p. 66) was told: "You are learning much in the spirit world with him. They are trying to arrange for you to *remember* snatches of what you see there. For this reason, they often waken you during the night in the hope that you will remember what you have just seen."

The "communicator" of S. Bedford (*Death—an*

Interesting Journey, Alcuin Press Ltd., p. 114) made two references to this matter. In one he said what many others have said, namely, that when a child dies the mother contacts him during deep sleep. He observed, "When waking up [=re-entering the 'blinkers'-like physical body], *the mother would have no recollection of these meetings*, except, perhaps, memory of an occasional 'dream' about her child. Yet her meetings with her child have been recorded in her Soul memory. When she, in turn, 'passes over', there is her child to meet her and recognition is immediate". He also said (p. 137): "Sometimes in our sleep the soul travels to the spirit world [='Paradise'], attracted by love. On these rare occasions we are in such *a deep sleep* that we seldom dream. If we were able to *remember* these reunions in the spirit world, it would interfere with our life on earth".

5. STATEMENTS OF PSYCHICAL RESEARCHERS, ETC.

The statements of the pseudo-dead, of astral projectors, of psychics and of "communicators" are at least reasonable when we note that many psychical researchers have concluded that telepathy is going on between mortals at all times, yet we are unaware of (do not "remember") the fact. Similarly, a person who awakens from hypnosis may fail to "remember" anything that has transpired.

ACKNOWLEDGEMENTS

For permission to make brief extracts from copyright material the writer tenders grateful thanks to the following publishers and authors:

A.S.P.R., X, 1916, p. 7.

Alcuin Press Ltd.: S. Bedford, *Death—an Interesting Journey*, p. 114.

Alfred A. Knopf: Wilfred Brandon, *Open the Door*, 1935, pp. xviii, 97, 137.

Andrew Dakers Ltd.: Dr Alice Gilbert, *Philip in Two Worlds*, 1948, p. 94.

Aquarian Press: Dr Alice Gilbert, *Philip in the Spheres*, 1952, pp. 17, 56, 101. Robert Crookall, *The Study and Practice of Astral Projection*, 1961, pp. 8, 64, 73, 103.

Arthurs Press Ltd.: Dr Nandor Fodor, *Encyclopedia of Psychic Science*, 1933, p. 207.

Arrowsmith Ltd.: Mrs C. A. Dawson-Scott, *From Four Who are Dead*, 1926, pp. 13–19.

C. W. Daniel & Co. Ltd.: Olive C. B. Pixley, *The Trail*; "A.B.", *One Step Higher*, 1937, p. 38.

Charles Taylor: F. Heslop, *Speaking Across the Border-line*, 1912, pp. 11, 24, 28, 61; *Further Messages Across the Border-line*, 1921, p. 67.

Colbey & Rich Ltd.: Dr J. M. Peebles, *Immortality*, 1883, p. 149.

Collins & Co. Ltd.: The Revd. C. Drayton Thomas, *Life Beyond Death with Evidence*, 1928, pp. 20, 78.

Constable & Co. Ltd.: Doris and Hilary Severn, *In the Next Room*, 1911, p. 29.

Creative Age Press: Mrs Eileen J. Garrett, *Telepathy*, 1941, p. 93.

Curtiss: A. C. and F. H. Curtiss, *Realms of the Living Dead*, 1917, pp. 61, 92, 111.

C. W. Daniel & Co. Ltd.: Constance Wiley, *A Star of Hope*, 1938, pp. 56, 75.

Daily Mail: November 30th, 1959.

David Stott: Anon., *I Awoke*, 1895, pp. 36, 39.

Dunstant: *Letters from Lancelot*, 1931.

E. W. Allen: Anon., *Life Beyond the Grave*, 1876, pp. 34, 40, 96.

Elliott: Revd. G. Maurice Elliott, *Angels Seen Today*, 1919, p. 10.

English Universities Press Ltd.: Dr R. C. Johnson, *Psychical Research*, 1955, p. 136.

Felsberg: Fr. J. Greber, *Communication with the Spirit World*, 1932, p. 112.

Fernie: "Friend H!!!", *The Dead—Active!*, 1919, pp. 21, 119.

G. Bell & Sons Ltd.: Zoë Richmond, *Evidence of Purpose*, 1938, p. 53; Dorothy Grenside, *The Meaning of Dreams*, 1923, p. 117.

George Allen & Unwin Ltd.: E. C. Randall, *The Dead Have Never Died*, 1918, p. 65; *Frontiers of After Life*, 1922, pp. 46, 154.

George G. Harrap: Dr Horatio Dresser, *The Open Vision*, p. 333.

Gollancz: Katherine Trevelyan, *Fool in Love*, 1960, p. 215.

Grant Richards: Revd. C. L. Tweedale, *Man's Survival After Death*, 1909.

Harper Bros.: Arthur Ford, *Nothing So Strange*, 1958, pp. 164, 225, 246; Margaret Cameron, *The Seven Purposes*, 1918, p. 299.

Hillside Press Ltd.: W. S. Montgomery Smith, *Life and Work in the Spiritual Body*, pp. 14, 64, 87.

Hoey: M. Hoey, *Truths from the Spirit World*, 1907, pp. 50, 97, 122.

Hutchinson & Co. Ltd.: Robert Crookall, *The Supreme Adventure*, 1961, pp. 161, 238.

J. Burns: Mrs Cora L. V. Tappan, *Discourses*, 1875, pp. 41, 69.

John Murray: Mary E. Monteith, *The Fringe of Immortality*, 1920, pp. 6, 146, 195.

Journ. Friends' Historic Society: 1923.

Kegan Paul, Tench, Trubner & Co. Ltd.: P. E. Cornillier, *The Survival of the Soul*, 1921, pp. 198, 290, 314, 412; Hereward Carrington, *Your Psychic Powers*, 1920, p. 57; E. Gurney, F. W. H. Myers and F. Podmore, *Phantasms of the Living*, 1886; Professor G. Henslow, *Proofs of the Truths of Spiritualism*, 1919, p. 48.

L.S.A. Publications Ltd.: E. A. Tietkens, *Mediumistic and Psychical Experiences;* Mrs G. Vivien, b.a., *Love Conquers Death*, p. 61; Olive B. Pixley, *Listening In*, p. 2.

Light: LV, p. 86; LXV, p. 86; LXXXX, p. 16; LXXXII, p. 40.

Longmans Green & Co. Ltd.: F. W. H. Myers, *Human Personality and its Survival of Bodily Death*, 1907, pp. 238, 245, 332; Lady Barrett, *Personality Survives Death*, 1937, p. 113.

Lucis Publishing Co. Ltd.: Alice A. Bailey, *The Externalisation of the Heirarchy*, 1958.

Macmillan & Co. Ltd.: Archbishop William Temple, *Nature, Man and God*, p. 457.

Methuen & Co. Ltd.: Mrs Kelway Bamber, *Claude's Second Book*, 1919, p. 121.

Philip Allen & Co. Ltd.: Kate Wingfield, *Guidance from Beyond*, 1923, p. 35; *More Guidance from Beyond*, 1925, pp. 12, 13.

Prediction: August 1961, p. 17.

Psychic Book Club: Mrs Kelway Bamber, *Claude's Book*, 1918, p. 49; Mrs Gladys Osborn Leonard, *The Last Crossing*, 1937, p. 73.

Psychic Press Ltd.: Geraldine Cummins, *Travellers in Eternity*, 1948, pp. 171, 177; Revd. C. Drayton Thomas, *Precognition and Human Survival*, p. 80; W. S. Montgomery Smith, *Light in Our Darkness*, 1926, p. 43; G. Trevor, *Death's Door Opens*, 1950, p. 30.

Quart. Trans. B.C.P.S., V, 1926, p. 58.

Rider & Co. Ltd.: Elsa Barker, *Letters from a Living Dead Man*, 1914, pp. 22, 120, 235, 243, 253, 285, 286; H. M. Nathan, *Man's Cosmic Horizon*; Mabel Beatty, *The Temple of the Body*, p. 72; Kamatini, *The Soul's Journeys*; Geoffrey Hodson, *The Science of Seership*, p. 130; Lord Dowding, *Lychgate*, 1945, pp. 13, 26, 50, 60; J. Arthur Findlay, *On the Edge of the Etheric*, *The Rock of Truth*; Mrs Annie Brittain, *'Twixt Earth and Heaven*, p. 86; Mrs H. S. Smith, *Voices from the Void*; Geraldine Cummins, *Unseen Numbers*, 1951, p. 121; Jane Sherwood, *The Psychic Bridge*, p. 31; Léon Denis, *Here and Hereafter*, 1910, p. 252; Mrs Rhys David, *What is Your Will?*, pp. 67, 218; W. S. Montgomery Smith, *Two Worlds Are Ours*, p. 143.

Rinehart & Co. (New York): Dr Sherwood Eddy, *You Will Survive After Death*, 1950.

S.P.R.: *Journ.*, 1908, 1895, 1960, pp. 276, 283; *Proc.*, VI, p. 17, XXXV, 1, 1960, pp. 119, 122.

Sidgwick & Jackson Ltd.: W. H. Salter, *Zoar*, 1961, pp. 184, 204.

Society of Communion: G. Welsford, *Key of Gold*.

Spiritual Frontiers Fellowship: Vol. vii, 1962, p. 3.

Stott, David: Anon, *I Awoke*, pp. 24, 36, 96, 126.

Theosophical Publishing House: Dr Annie Besant, *Man's Life in This and Other Worlds*, 1913, p. 42; C. W. Leadbeater, *Invisible Helpers*, 3rd ed., 1917; Phoebe D. Bendit and Dr L. J. Bendit, *Man Incarnate*, 1957.

Vincent Stuart: Margaret Eyre, *The Revealing Light*, 1962, pp. 19–20, 64, 89.

W. J. Sinkins: A. Farnese, *A Wanderer in the Spirit Lands*, 1896, p. 25.

Watkins & Co. Ltd.: G. G. André, *Morning Talks with Spirit Friends*, 1926, pp. 89, 124; Mary Bruce Wallace, *The Coming Light*, 1924, p. 19; Mary Wright Sewall, *Neither Dead Nor Sleeping*, 1921, pp. 10, 304; Anon., *Letters from the Other Side*, 1919, pp. 2, 13, 14, 79, 311, 145–51, Major W. T. Pole, *Private Dowding*, 1917, pp. 75, 98; Professor E. Bozzano, *Discarnate Influence on Human Life*; 1938.